NO DRAGONS HERE

Every blessing,
Roberta Moore

NO DRAGONS HERE

AND OTHER STORIES

ROBERTA MOORE

AMBASSADOR INTERNATIONAL
GREENVILLE, SOUTH CAROLINA & BELFAST, NORTHERN IRELAND

www.ambassador-international.com

No Dragons Here
And other Stories

Copyright 2011 - Roberta Moore
All rights reserved

ISBN: 978-1-935507-7-55

Printed by Bethel Solutions

Ambassador International
Emerald House
427 Wade Hampton Blvd
Greenville, SC 29609, USA

Ambassador Books and Media
The Mount
2 Woodstock Link
Belfast, BT6 8DD, Northern Ireland, UK

www.ambassador-international.com

The colophon is a trademark of Ambassador

CONTENTS

HOW IT CAME ABOUT

It is neither the reason for my visit nor what was said that I can remember; it is the comfortable sofa, the warmth from the smiles and the oil burning stove; the cup of tea. Many times I had passed this large, square, yellow building set at the end of a short curved driveway, with its shiny windows looking down over the Bann Valley and far across to the Derry Hills. In spring I used to look into the garden and wonder at the masses of purple and yellow crocuses among the enormous trees. I had been brought up in this district of County Antrim, attended Finvoy Presbyterian Church all of my life, but it was not until I was 24 years old that I had found myself inside our church manse.

I continued along the twisting, turning path of life, aiming to follow God's sure and steady leading. Of the many incidents, people and circumstances which have left firm traces on my heart, two have become of particular significance: I married a Presbyterian minister, Drew Moore, and I read a book relating the work of Rev Bill Jackson with the Presbyterian Church in Malawi.

After living in a manse for 25 years and visiting Malawi several times I came to three decisions: to find out more about the history of our manses, to discover stories from within our manses, and to bring these together in print.

This book contains true stories. The adventures encountered in their collection are a story-book in themselves. Some stories needed minor tinkering for clear understanding. The nature of telling may not always be as you would expect, but what does that matter as long as you enjoy them?

ACKNOWLEDGEMENTS

I am grateful to God for calling me to be part of the World-wide Church of Christ. I owe thanks to my husband Drew who encouraged me to continue with this venture, to my sister Ruby who gave many hours to advise and edit, and to the two young watercolour artists, Zion K. Chirwa and David G. Moore. I wish to thank the many other people in Malawi and Ireland who encouraged and assisted me in many ways. Open invitations were issued by various means to all areas of Ireland and Malawi for folk to supply stories; a special thanks is due to those who responded by contributing their story --- without them there would be no book! Unfortunately it was not possible to include all the material. Every effort has been made to check facts as well as place and personal name spelling. Please accept my apologies for any inadvertent errors.

Help was also received from several books, articles or web sites:

"A History of Presbyterianism in Ireland" RevT.Hamilton, published by T and T Clark.

"A Short History of Ireland" Sean McMahon, published by Irish Books and Media.

"An Outline History of the Congregation of First Presbyterian Church, Lurgan 1684-1966" printed by L.M.Press Ltd, Lurgan.

"Ballyroney, Its Church and People" John William Lockington.

"Ecclesiastical History of Ireland: from the earliest times to the Present Time" W. Doole Killen, published by Macmillan, London.

"History of the Presbyterian Church in Ireland" J.S. Reid, published by Kessinger Publishing.

"Into All the World" Edited by Jack Thompson, published by

the Overseas Board of the Presbyterian Church in Ireland.

"Laws of Livingstonia" W.P.Livingstone, published by Hodder and Stoughton.

"Send us Friends" Ted Jackson.

"Short History of the Presbyterian Church in Ireland" Prof. John M. Barkley, published by Publishing Board of Presbyterian Church in Ireland.

www.firstchurchbelfast.com

UNTOLD STORIES

I tramped once, under a hot February sun, through the undergrowth in the Karoo region of South Africa towards a cave.

My eyes were guided upwards to scan the surface of a huge rocky outcrop partly hidden by creepers and shrubs.

A passer by could have travelled that way, even to within a few feet of that rock, and been completely ignorant of what was revealed there.

Red figures had been painted on the surface. They were the testimony of Bushmen whose home that place had been. The small magenta motifs were not static or solitary. They were active, interacting with their environment: some were running with arrows, some were gathered in groups, tending their animals; fighting battles; eating and drinking.

A few years ago I slid down the river Nile on a boat towards the Valley of the Kings. On each bank was a narrow strip of green where farmers were growing crops round their small simple dwellings. Children played and laughed at the edge of the river, waving and shouting as we passed. The sun was burning and the staff on the SS Helio were more than courteous. Stepping ashore we picked our way up the fiery hot sandy hillside, and then down through a cool narrow doorway into the tombs of a pharaoh from long ago. On the walls of that vast chamber were exquisite pictures in stunning colours depicting the story of that great pharaoh in life and death. On other days we explored the ancient temples and unbelievably massive obelisks, their surfaces embellished with characters and pictures proclaiming the adventures of those who had lived and worked there.

Wherever people have lived stories have unfolded and many of these are still untold. Often two countries, though far distant from each other, have found some common story ground. Two such countries are Ireland, a tiny square of land hanging on the edge of the Atlantic Ocean, and Malawi, of almost equal size, tucked away in the African Rift Valley. The Church of Christ has been planted there and Presbyterian manses have been built up and down our lands. Imagine if those manse walls were covered with red figures or scratched characters sketching untold stories over the centuries, what would be revealed?

From Ballymena to Bandawe, Carrickfergus to Karonga, New-mills to Nkhata Bay, and Malahide to Mzuzu, no wall, no matter how vast, would be able to hold all the pictures needed to illustrate the complete stories of the Presbyterian Manses in Ireland and Malawi.

Before we listen at the keyhole or peep through to share snippets of recorded scenes we should stand tall and cast our eyes back over the years.

What circumstances surrounded the Presbyterians first coming to our lands? How, when and where were the first manses built and who laid the pathway spanning thousands of miles that links the manses, ministers, churches and peoples of the Emerald Isle with their partners in the Warm Heart of Africa?

Where did these stories begin?

A BED, A TABLE, A CHAIR AND A LAMP

If we consider the relationship between congregation and minister coming together in the manse it draws to mind a story from the Bible in 2 Kings Chapter 4. A lady and her husband from Shumen provided a base for the prophet Elisha, from where he could carry on the work of God. The couple made a little room and lovingly furnished it with a bed, a chair, a table and a lamp. Through the ministry of Elisha, under God, great blessing came to that Shunammite home.

Think for a moment of this parable: the Shunammite lady and her husband as the local Church; the provided accommodation as the manse; the prophet as the parish minister. What a wonderful picture of how congregation and minister, dependant on and serving each other, can bring glory to God. The story in 2 Kings has great joy but also moments of sadness, frustration, uncertainty and distress. So too have these stories collected from the manses of Ireland and Malawi.

STORIES FROM IRELAND

The Gospel was most famously brought to Irish soil a mere 432 years after the time of Christ by a Latin-speaking slave turned missionary, Patrick.

Pictures on the saintly walls surrounding Patrick are blurred and appear to record more fiction than fact, but he left a stamp of the cross on Irish soil and things moved on.

Scampering down succeeding centuries in Ireland, we might catch glimpses of monastic settlements; stone beehive houses; Viking warriors and great battle scenes where Brian, King of all Ireland, reigned with Christian conscience. Walls throughout the island would whisper to us stories of saints and scholars; motte and bailey fortresses of Norman knights could unloose many an adventure and reveal the mark of many an axe.

With slowing steps, 1000 years after Patrick walked Irish soil, if we take time to look, we would spot men who confess the Presbyterian theology begin to make faint scratchings on Irish walls. In the city of Dublin, the first university of the land was Trinity College and there, making his mark as the first Vice Chancellor, was Rev Walter Travers – a Presbyterian minister.

After another six centuries, up in the north of the island, if we walk six miles towards Larne from the 12th century Carrickfergus castle on the northern shore of Belfast Lough, we would find a few thatched cottages making up the village of Ballycarry. It was to this quiet rural place that Rev Edward Brice came from Scotland across the Irish Sea to start the first Presbyterian ministry in the Emerald Isle.

Other men followed Mr Brice and so little groups of Presbyterian worshippers gathered here and there.

We can catch no sight of manses yet, but we can hear God's Word preached with power and perceive the lives of people changed by Him. If we continue looking we will begin to notice gloomy clouds gather to cast a shadow across the picture and the peoples' faces show strong resolve as blows of persecution fall. Attempts to banish all Presbyterians from the land almost succeeded but in the year 1642 a turn of events brought change.

The Irish were in rebellion, living up to their apparently inherent inclination to division, and a Scottish regiment under Major General Munroe landed at Carrickfergus to quell the fighting. There were among them Presbyterian ministers who served the ranks as Chaplains. When peace came, as peace does after storms, the Chaplains stayed behind and formed the first church Presbytery with ruling elders. The Presbyterian Church was born in Ireland. It grew, till after twenty years we can count eighty congregations, seventy ministers serving and some small signs of homes provided for those early clergy.

At Ballyclare in 1655, Rev Gilbert Simpson was given the princely sum of £20 to build a manse. Peering closely at the stone walls of that manse and other houses of the time, we can imagine them covered with deep chiselled carvings depicting dark days and frightening nights of renewed persecution – worshippers huddled in barns and at the back of thorny hedges; church buildings bolted up; homes with broken windows, empty rooms and signs of speedy escapes; clergymen separated from their families crouching in prison cells; and in the dimness of those lean church years our reluctant eyes can also, here and there, detect huddled groups of ministers squabbling among themselves. Through the turmoil the light of God still filters and as it is allowed to shine the darkness clears away to show us men rising up and congregations springing into fresh new life.

Travelling by coach, shank's mare or pony, along the shores of Belfast Lough we come upon a smallish town of half a dozen streets and several hundred houses built of bricks made from the lough shore mud. Stopping a while we may well encounter Rev James McBride who had been called in 1695 from Clare to serve the church in this settlement of Belfast. He would be overjoyed to show us the brand new church and manse in Rosemary Lane built on land donated by the Marquis of Donegal – at the persuasion of McBride himself. If we return to visit at another time some ten years later, turn the manse doorknob, venture inside and creep upstairs to the master's bedroom we will find the mark of a thrust sword upon the wall. The rather unorthodox minister had upset his fellow presbyters who sent the Sovereign of Belfast to procure his arrest. The Sovereign's attack was keen and swift but his rapier pierced only a portrait of the clergyman, who had meantime escaped to Scotland, to return and preach another day!

Times in Ireland were hard in the 1700s. As we shelter under thatched roofs and scan the thick mud walls we might see images of grain being reaped by sickle; men hand ploughing their patches of ground; tired, worn women pulling the harsh flax; families gathered to eat their daily meal of potatoes, milk and oatmeal. We would see thousands of worn out folk handing over three pounds fifty pence to clamber aboard shabby ships heading for America. We would see fighting and bloodshed and if we look closely we can recognise one or two figures: a Presbyterian minister, Rev Samuel Morrell, shot and falling amidst an angry crowd of rioters; further on the sad and sorry sight of Rev James Porter being hanged "until dead" for his part in the political uprising of 1798.

God's light had not however been extinguished and brighter days would still dawn for country and Church.

We should visit a house at Greenfield towards Ballyroney among the drumlins of County Down, against the backdrop of the Mournes. Those walls could show the figure of Rev William Fletcher, who came to minister at Ballyroney in 1783, grinding grain at the local mill, with a look of urgency on his youthful face because in the first years of his ministry there, he was a tenant in that house and had to pay a fine of ten and sixpence for every barrel of grain he ground elsewhere! Whether Mr Fletcher grew tired of this arrangement we can only guess, but he in due course bought the house himself and thereafter it served well as the manse for many years to come.

1840 was a grand and memorable year for Irish Presbyterian churches - upon her walls are etched the memory of two groups of men, who for long years had stood apart, now sitting close together, hands outstretched: the Secession and the Ulster Synods. They met and united as the Presbyterian Church in Ireland with the total of 433 congregations. Along with unity came sending - to take the name of Jesus, His love and His work to other lands. The first to be sent were Rev James Glasgow and Rev Alexander Kerr with their wives. They were called to India, sailed for Bombay and then travelled the strange mysterious dusty journey north to Saurashtra, the peninsula of Gujarat, surrounded by the Arabian sea, to begin their work. It was good work, well done, but, in those days before the use of prophylactic medicines, the cost to them was high – the young daughter of Rev and Mrs. J. Glasgow, and Rev A. Kerr both fell ill, died and were buried there. Those remaining carried on the work and others joined them.

Soon sickness and death were also too common in the island they had left behind. The walls of manses and almost every other home in Ireland would force our eyes to look at scenes of hunger, poverty and loss as the dreadful figure of famine strode across the Irish canvas. Pictures of starvation are not pleasant but they are real and they are forged forever not just on the walls but on the hearts and minds of Ireland.

Life for those who survived went on and life in the church grew stronger. Not all the congregations had a minister, and very few were able to provide a manse, so the Church took things in hand, worked out a plan and set up a Manse Fund which resulted in such a flurry of building work that after fifty years almost 400 manses were completed.

What human stories were lived out inside those manses is difficult to tell because their walls are mostly stony silent and almost bare of pictures. There must have been somewhere praying hands, willing hearts and ever ready feet, for, in the coming years, from manses and congregations up and down the land many did as Revs Kerr and Glasgow had done -- they set out from the shores of Ireland to share in the work of the Gospel in India, Syria, Austria, Italy, Lebanon, Israel, China, Spain, Jamaica, and eventually – Malawi!

Recently, however, some snapshots have been captured, some stories told: stories of explosions, dragons, and policemen; stories of dilemma, surprise and deceit; stories that warm the heart, stories that bring back memories and stories that make you laugh.

North Antrim Coast

AN UNEXPECTED GUEST

When we came to take up the work of Church Extension at Hazlebank Presbyterian Church in Coleraine, we did not have a manse in which to live.

"Look for a house in the district near to the church and buy it for the Church Extension Committee," I was told. We did as we were told, and found a suitable modern house at 8 Cairnmount Park, off the Ballycairn Road, just a mile from the fledgling Church.

Before coming to Coleraine, the Lord Jesus had given my wife and me a promise found in John 14v43: "If anyone loves me he will obey my teaching, my father will love him and We will come to him and make Our home with him." What a promise! In the Bible, Jesus says that He wants to make His dwelling with those who love Him: His love for us constrained us to take His Word far more seriously than ever before. If we love a person, we cherish, honour, and respect their words, wishes and claims on us; we consider them holy and binding.

Della and I wished to abide in Christ and we prayed that God would live with us, in our new manse. The house had to be refurbished, so we set about getting bits and pieces of carpets and curtains.

I remember one evening; we were putting down a piece of new carpet along the hall floor. As we were down on our knees, measuring and cutting the carpet to size, I said to Della my wife, "You know, we have not prayed about the hallway and entrance into our new home." We stopped to pray on our knees on the floor; we asked God to help us both to respond with love and sympathy and compassion to any who would come to the manse door, and that the Lord would begin to show us how He was going to make the manse a welcome dwelling place for Himself.

During our ministry in Clough and Seaford we had both experienced God's gift of the Holy Spirit. This brought us to repentance over our failure to follow Jesus uncompromisingly, and consequently there was a change in our lifestyle; we were to take the commands of Jesus and make them obligatory for ourselves, and we would often pray "Lord make your dwelling in us."

Some weeks after we had made our new manse quite comfortable, on a wet stormy night, the door bell rang, and there standing in the rain was a mother and child. I invited her and her child to come into the lighted hallway, and noticed some bruising on her face. She was frightened and embarrassed at calling at such a late hour. She had been attacked by her drunken husband, and for her safety and that of her child, she thought it best to leave home and come to the new minister's home. So our visitors were put up in the manse guest room and spent three weeks with us until we were able to help her to sort out her domestic situation.

Two abiding memories remain of that first of many visitors whom the Lord sent to 8 Cairnmount Park: The Lord tested us on that prayer we prayed when we were down on our knees on that hallway carpet; we had told the Lord it was His house and we would take in any He would send. He had sent and we had received.

After a week or so in the manse that lady kept on saying, "It is so peaceful in this house; I wish my home had this atmosphere." So Christ had come to dwell with us in the guise of a frightened mother and her child, and we were again reminded of scripture in Matthew 10v 41: "This is a large work I have called you into, but do not be overwhelmed by it. It is best to start small; give a cup of cold water to someone who is thirsty, for instance; the smallest act of giving or receiving makes you a true apprentice, you will not lose out on a thing."

As I look back over the years, we can only praise GOD for His faithfulness.

Rev Sam Millar

A CUP OF COLD WATER

The door bell of Hill St Manse, Lurgan, must have rung thousands of times during the twenty years we lived there, but only relatively few of them stand out clearly in my mind.

On one particular afternoon, about 4.30, I recall exactly what I was doing when that familiar chime sounded: I was standing in front of the black and chrome electric cooker prodding sausages as they sizzled in the pan, while the potatoes were boiling on the back burner; our youngest daughter Hannah was in her high chair, to my left, near the window which looked out to the back garden and the small wooded area beyond. The table was set for tea in readiness for my husband's return from his afternoon of pastoral visiting.

Through the small square hatch in the wall to the right of the cooker, I could see the other children playing on the living room floor. Often if they wanted to avoid being seen they would close the hatch and fasten it closed from behind!

As the chimes faded I made my way from the kitchen, down the pink-carpeted hall, past the stairs, to the front porch. As I opened the inner glass door, I could see, standing on the other side of the outer glass door, a young man of about thirty or maybe less. There was nothing unusual about his appearance; I cannot recall his facial features. When I opened the door he spoke pleasantly enough, but it was clear he was not a local man. He inquired if this was the residence of Rev Drew Moore; when I confirmed this he introduced himself, although I cannot remember his name, explaining that he was in need of a little help. After a sentence or two when it became clear that he was embarking on a long involved tale I was not at all sure how to react. I clearly remember thinking to myself,

"I don't know this man, if he is telling the truth, or if it is safe to bring him into our home".

However, as quickly as this thought had passed through my mind it was followed by the hint of words from Matthew's gospel: "If anyone gives even a cup of cold water to one of these …"

So I quickly reasoned that if help was needed, and after all, the stranger appeared to know my husband, then at least I should invite him in and listen to his story.

In the kitchen my visitor immediately seated himself at the side of our wooden table near the cooker. I made a cup of tea, setting it, together with a plate of biscuits, on the table.

The young man related how he was a member of a Presbyterian Church in Larne where he helped with the Youth Work; to-day he had travelled from Larne to Lurgan to visit his mother but when he arrived she was not at home, which was unfortunate, not only because he had looked forward to seeing her but also because he had brought with him only enough money for his train fare to Lurgan, depending on his mother to supply a meal and the funds for his return journey. By this stage my sausages were cooked more than enough, the biscuits were finished and it was becoming clear that the help needed was financial.

My guest could see I was hesitating; he assured me that if I could supply his need he would surely make plans to repay me in full; in fact within a few minutes he suggested that on the next visit to his mother, he would return the money, in a marked envelope, leaving it in a well known Travel Agent shop in the centre of Lurgan.

As I was turning all of this over in my mind while attempting to carry on a conversation, the idea came to me that perhaps I should make an excuse to go into the study then phone the minister of the church in Larne to verify the story I had just heard. Immediately I rebuked myself for my cynicism and thought again of "The Cup of Water." I was swayed. I went to my purse, opened it, and handed over the required amount—with a bit extra for possible emergencies. I'm sure my hand trembled slightly as I handed over the money.

I saw my guest to the front door where he offered his thanks then walked down the front driveway, disappeared round the gate post, turning right towards the town centre. As the door closed I headed into the study, thumbed through the register of ministers' telephone numbers in the Blue Book and dialled a number. Our brother minister answered his call in Larne; it took only a few words of explanation from me for him to assure me that I had indeed been the latest victim of a known con man whose favourite target seemed to be Presbyterian manses. If it was any consolation, I was told, it was best that I had handed over the money because on one fateful occasion when it had been refused, the hostess was attacked and robbed.

So, as always, God had used His Word for my good and perhaps some day, if it has not already happened, the sharp edge of His Word will be used to bring that young man to faith in Jesus and his life will be transformed for good.

Roberta Moore

North Antrim Coast

AN ANGEL HAD COME

It was heading into our first winter in Mountjoy Manse, near Omagh, when I discovered the shed half filled with fire-logs.

"John, did you put sticks in our shed?"

"No", replied the neighbour as he continued sawing at the tree he had recovered from recent storm damage.

The following Sunday morning:

"Maurice, did you deliver logs to our house?"

"No," came his curious melodic reply. "I know you were looking for fire wood but I didn't get any, sorry."

"John," (that's a different John. We seem to have a lot of Johns about Co Tyrone) "John, were you responsible for putting logs in my shed? Someone left firewood in the shed at the manse and I would need to pay and I don't know who I owe it to. Was it you?"

Once again the answer was "No."

What was I to do? Accept what was an apparent gift, or keep on looking for a kind person who left me logs for the fire and was owed money?

You see part of the difficulty was, I had made it known on several visits that I would like to know where to get good fire wood. Several suggestions had been made but I hadn't followed up any before finding the load of wood in the shed.

Weeks passed with the mystery unsolved. I had to conclude an angel had come. The thought of someone being owed money for services rendered was too much to bear.

As the story was told and the questions asked there was no other feasible explanation. A divine messenger, an angel or someone acting out of Christian kindness, has responded to the new minister's request with a link-box full of logs. Some good Samaritan has come and gone and hadn't sought any reward. An angel with a chainshaw and an axe.

The logs burned quite well, albeit a few needed seasoned, but one cannot complain, a gift after all is a gift.

December came; I had just put a few logs on the fire one damp Thursday evening when there was a knock at the door: I opened it.

"Were the logs alright for you yer Reverence?"

I nodded.

"That'll be £20 then."

"So it was you, Mr Temple, you're the angel!

"What do you mean?"

So I briefly recounted my presumption that an angel had come. He left puzzled.

Rev K. Nelson

North Antrim Coast

TWO BROTHERS

It was 11.30 p.m. on a Saturday night. I had just finished preparing the children's address for the Sunday morning service in Toberkeigh Church. I was watching "Match of the Day" when there was a loud knock at the front door. My immediate thought was "Who could that be at this time of the night?" As I opened the door a young man called Kenneth, who was not a regular church-goer, walked past me, uttering the words, "I'm here to see about getting saved." He was ushered into the living room. Over in the corner our young baby, Thomas, was asleep in his cot. Kenneth and I conversed until well after mid-night, and I suppose, not wanting to encourage a spur-of-the-moment profession of faith which would not be lasting, I suggested that my young friend should go home and think over what we had discussed. What a rebuke I received when he replied, "I was ill in hospital six months ago and have thought of nothing but this ever since. That's why I'm here." There and then he came to put his faith in Christ.

Imagining that he had walked the couple of miles round to the manse, I offered him a lift home. However, he informed me that his father (who did not openly profess faith) had not only driven him here and was still in the car at the front door, but was the one who had encouraged him to seek help from the minister. Perhaps that said more about the father than he even knew about himself! Father was immediately invited in and supper provided at 1.00a.m. amid much happy conversation!

It has been my practice to allow a new convert time to make known to others what has taken place, and so it was three weeks before I called at the young man's home to see how things were with him. Following my visit, I was accompanied to my car by Kenneth's younger brother, Mark, and what a joy it was to be told by him, "I too have become a Christian."

Both these young men have gone on to become mature Christian believers, and Mark is now a Presbyterian Chaplain with the British Army.

Rev T.A. Moore

This manse was demolished in 1985 and a single-story manse erected in its place. During the demolition and building period the Moore family was housed in a disused farmhouse belonging to a member of the congregation.

North Antrim Coast

ONCERS

My father was the minister of a large city congregation and I was born in the manse about 10.30 on a Sunday morning. I was told that my father took the service in the church that day – there was no such thing as paternity leave! – however, this illustrates the place of the church both in our home and our lives.

The manse was a rambling three story house with sixty stairs from the ground up to the attic. We were very aware of these stairs, as we were sent "to the attic and back" if we misbehaved.

There was one coal fire in the living room; in cold weather if one sat near the fire it was warm enough, but for anyone at the back of the room or in another room the temperature was several degrees lower! As the youngest in the family I usually ended up near the back.

An important item in our house was our father's bicycle! He cycled everywhere on it in all weathers: to church, to meetings, and visiting the five hundred families connected to our congregation once a year as well as visits to hospitals and a host of other duties.

My father's study in our house was a place set apart. We were expected to keep quiet and if any visitor had called on him, we were to be seen but not heard. Assistant ministers would visit frequently and we accepted each of these young men into our home as part of our family. One very sad occasion that I recall concerned a young man who had been our assistant for a number of years. Soon after he had received a call to a congregation we were very shocked to hear that he became seriously ill and died a short time later. Even though I was a young lad at the time this had a very big effect on me.

As "children of the manse" we were expected to behave per-fectly in church. In our congregation there were two services every Sunday, one in the morning and one in the evening. On one occasion two elderly ladies remarked to my mother that her children were just "oncers" at church, meaning that we attended only one service each Sunday. The same ladies were seemingly unaware that they themselves attended evening service only!

All in all our family life in the manse was a happy one in spite of living conditions being much simpler and more basic in style than at present.

North Antrim Coast

A MANSE CHILDHOOD

My earliest memory of growing up in West Church Manse, Bangor – the freezing winter of 1962! I was four years old, and my months-old baby brother, Andrew, seemed to wheeze and cough incessantly. My job was to wheel him up and down in his pram (I could reach the pram handle, and felt very grown-up and responsible), while mum got on with the chores. We had no central heating in those days: not a trial for me but a sore one for our visitor that winter, the diminutive Gujarati pastor, S.D. Parmar ("kaka", or uncle to me). I adored him, my four year old self blissfully unaware that he was totally culture shocked and quite unable to cope with the severe weather.

He was one of a long procession of visitors; some came for hours, some days, some weeks or even months. West Church Manse was an open house; I assumed that this was normal, I suppose, until I grew older and became aware that not everyone lived in this manner. At times my siblings and I may have resented this somewhat (I remember with a pang of thirty year old guilt, adding salt to one visitor's cup of coffee… but this particular gentleman *did* visit every day, including Christmas day, for years on end!)

In retrospect, however, I think I gained much more than I lost; we were exposed to such a wide variety of interesting and colourful characters and learned from a very young age to empathise with a heterogeneous mix of people.

Some of the most memorable included Lillias Dodds, a formidable but kindly missionary from China, with a deep voice. There was also Miss Margaret Zimmerer (or Tante M.), another indomitable lady, A German Catholic journalist who bravely decided to live in a council house in Ballymurphy at the height of the 1970's troubles and used to flee to the Manse for refuge when the bin-lid protests and army searches became unbearable. She used to enjoy a tot of good brandy (I don't blame her in the circumstances!); if you saw your former minister's wife scurrying into an off-licence in search of strong drink back then, it was under orders from the imperious Tante M.!

An extremely frequent visitor for years (daily in fact) was James Charles Alton, the son of a former provost at Trinity College, Dublin. J.C. had suffered a mental breakdown when young, but we could all see that he had been a brilliant student: his vocabulary was abstruse to the point of pedantry. He used to arrive regularly for coffee and shortbread, to read the Irish Times - and his Bible - whilst smoking a particularly noxious and evil-smelling pipe.

Members of the 1970's West Church congregation may remember Mr Alton sitting in the front row snoring sonorously throughout the service – except for the Lord's Prayer which he would enunciate loudly and at top speed in a frantic effort to reach Amen before everyone else.

In our early days of West Church, as well as general hospitality, a lot of meetings were held in the Manse. My bedroom was directly above the drawing room and I distinctly remember lying in bed struggling to go to sleep to the lusty hymn singing and the thump of the piano. "To GOD be the GLORY, great THINGS He has DONE!" I also remember my mother preparing endless sandwiches; as a child, in those un-PC days, I used to like to take the crusts she had cut off and pretend they were cigarettes, attempting to pout in film star fashion (this was the 1980's remember!)

There were occasional crises: the time(s) my father invited people for lunch and forgot to inform my mother, the time our Scottish terrier began demolishing the food for the "Three O'clock Club" tea party (this was a Senior Citizens' group) - even the time mum was stopped for speeding on her way back from morning service, rushing "to get the spuds on" for who knows how many guests. (The policeman let her off, by the way, but he didn't tell her).

I suppose it was only gradually that I found out that our domestic life wasn't totally "normal"; when I went to tea at a friend's house,

I was surprised when the phone didn't ring at least half a dozen times during the meal. We had, in those early days, a big house and garden, but very little spare cash compared to many of our peers; hand-me-down clothes, few outings, but a wonderful garden to play in, and Stricklands Glen and the seaside on our doorstep. And although I wanted to punch the child at primary school who rebuked me sanctimoniously for some minor misdemeanour, "I'm telling Miss, you shouldn't do that, you're a minister's daughter!" – I still look back on my manse childhood with enormous nostalgia, as a rich and very happy part of my life.

    Elizabeth Bailie

An excerpt from "West Church Bangor Onward Journey", published in 2009

North Antrim Coast

HENS AT GRANGE MANSE

I have now been retired for twenty six years but the following incident is still fresh in my memory. During my times at Grange congregation in the Ballymena Presbytery the garage was attached to the manse and behind it was an addition which had been used many years before for the minister to keep his horse. Evidently there were no cars in those days. Actually, while I was there, the manger was still in the wall of the room. On top of this room and the garage there was another room which was approached by stairs. Before we had a church hall this was where we had our weekly prayer meeting. Nothing unusual happened until I decided to keep a dozen hens in the room below.

A member of the congregation, whose job it was to buy and sell hens, kindly agreed to get me a dozen of the best fowl. There was no time set for delivery, but should I not be in when he arrived the man knew where to deposit the hens.

My world was turned upside down one Wednesday evening during the Prayer Meeting! My friend arrived, could see no sign of me and proceeded to "throw" the hens into the downstairs room.

An unholy row ensued and prayer was called to a halt! I, being a city man, was greatly embarrassed but the country members told me not to worry as they understood hens!

When the hens settled the prayer meeting continued as if nothing had happened. This did not mean, of course, that the event was forgotten; within the past year I was back at the church for an anniversary service and two of the older members reminded me of the night the hens came to the prayer meting!

P.S. The church now has a lovely new church hall and manse, minus the hens!

Rev Joe Mooney

THE CAT WHO CAME TO THE PRAYER MEETING

It was a Sunday evening and an older man was praying fervently in our front room. Suddenly he stopped and we heard him utter a loud "OOOH!" Next thing we heard his wife say calmly, "It's only the cat, Sammy!" Our cat had come into the room and decided that the gentleman's lap would be a first class, comfortable resting place!

It goes to show that it's advisable to pray with your eyes open!

THE MINISTER, THE POLICEMAN AND A PAIR OF EARRINGS

It was in the early eighties. Two types of men wore earrings; both were rather suspect. Either you were in the Duran Duran camp where the only requirement for adorning your ear was that the jewel matched the one in your brooch. Or you were rebelling against ....anything ... it did not really matter what as long as it was vaguely representative of the status quo.

My father *was* the status quo.

He embodied all that was law abiding and upright. He was slavishly punctual; took his responsibilities seriously to the point of obsession; rose every morning to face dutifully a new day full of deadlines, demands and discipleship. He was a Presbyterian minister and none I knew equalled his work ethic and desire to abide by the authorities.

The local community policeman often valued my father's contribution to routine enquiries; he was reliable, honest and had his ear to the ground: a fine upstanding member of the community. Mutual respect reigned supreme in their relationship. They knew where they were with each other.

My mother had, on a whim, bought a pair of clip-on stud earrings and had, in a moment of carelessness, lost one of the pair. Its partner lay on the kitchen windowsill until my teenage brother lifted it one day and wore it to provoke a reaction from my paternal grandmother, the same lady who had instilled the aforementioned values in my father. Having created a minor hullabaloo, the earring fell into the hands of my father who decided to play the same prank on my mother. So one Tuesday morning he clipped it on to his earlobe and waited until she had finished her upstairs cleaning. Five minutes later the doorbell rang. My father rushed to answer it, absent-mindedly forgetting the mischievous bauble in his ear. The policeman on the doorstep was welcomed and ushered into the room where the conversation was characteristically serious, confidential and of great import.

What was going on in that officer's head as he sat opposite this clerical-collared middle-aged man of the cloth, who represented all that was conventionally safe, and tried to avert his eyes from the modish silver stud winking at him from the noble earlobe?

We will never know. Was he intrigued to know whether he was sitting opposite a closet rebel or, worse still, a closet New Romantic? Was he expecting to return another day to find this slightly portly figure decked from head to toe in leathers – or lace?

When the policeman left my father returned to the kitchen where my mother was preparing lunch. When she turned round, her startled gasp immediately indicated that his prank had achieved its required, although admittedly delayed, result.

The realisation of the stir he had inadvertently caused dawned on my father --- and, do you know? --- I think he quite enjoyed speculating on the tea-break conversation in the Police Station and the possible notoriety it would bring in its wake!

THE BIG BANG

I arrived home after a morning's work around the parish, switched on the T.V. in the living- room, in preparation for watching the lunch time news, and proceeded to the kitchen to prepare a sandwich and a coffee.

The kettle had barely started boiling when there was what sounded like an earth-shattering explosion which seemed to shake the whole house. These were the days of The Troubles in Northern Ireland when bomb blasts in the towns and villages were relatively common. My instantaneous conclusion that a bomb had exploded down the street was, within a split second, set aside - in that I realised this was not some external event, but very definitely inside the manse.

With my mind racing and my heart thumping I returned to the kitchen doorway in fear and trepidation - by this stage surmising that my TV had exploded. At first those fears seemed confirmed, as, looking down the long hallway, I could see only a scene of utter devastation. The hall was filled with what I thought was smoke; as it began to settle, there was revealed a mass of ankle deep rubble strewn all over the hall carpet.

Before the dust had time to settle or I had enough time to interpret the evidence, the doorbell rang, and, without pausing, a visitor opened the front door and walked in. It was Eddie Kirk, the minister of the neighbouring Presbyterian Church in Portglenone – it was his normal custom to ring the bell and just walk on in! Instantly he took a step backwards in visible fear and confusion. As we stared at each other from opposite ends of the hallway through clouds of settling dust, and over heaps of rubble, he eventually stammered, "What are you doing?"

I was still too shell-shocked at that moment to think of a witty reply, as together we began to take in what had happened.

The huge (and heavy) lathe-and-plaster hall ceiling had hung on conscientiously for 120 years since the manse was first built – obviously slowly weakening with the passage of time. On this day it just could not hold on any longer and crashed to the ground, scattering about a ton of rubble on the hall carpet.

I have often wondered: if my neighbour had been five seconds earlier would I have been in charge of a vacancy?!

Certainly, at the very least, Eddie would have had a sore head!

Rev Albert Baxter
This manse built in Portglenone in 1872, was demolished in 1996, to be replaced by a new Manse, on the same site.

North Antrim Coast

THE PROTEST

The manse for Ballynure Presbyterian Church was built in the "Classical Presbyterian Manse" style and has stood since 1884.

We moved into the manse in April 2000 and had settled well, enjoying the incredible space that such a manse afforded a family, yet we were still blissfully unaware of what a winter holds for the occupants of a hundred year old building!

For a number of years we had holidayed in France with Euro-camp during July and the year 2000 was no different. We were in the Northern region, Pas-de-Calais. Meanwhile, at home, there was unrest.

Quite oblivious of what was going on we happened to be watching French T.V one evening. The headlines included stories and scenes of political and civil unrest across the roads of N.Ireland. There came on to the screen the picture of a large crowd blocking the road and there, looming in the background was a house we recognised --- Ballynure Manse! We nearly jumped out of our skins! We could scarcely believe it! A few of the protesters were interviewed, all the while with our home as a backdrop. The year 2000 was "The Year of Drumcree"*. On Sunday July 9th, after their annual Drumcree Road march, the Portadown Lodge* was barred from entering the mainly nationalist Garvaghy Road. The Lodge called for four hours of protests right across the province on the following day. However, protests and disturbances continued into Monday night. The A8 trunk road from Belfast to Larne was the focus for one such protest. Some 800 people gathered on Monday evening the 10th July to blockade the road, just at the top of the village of Ballynure, outside Ballynure Manse!

The rest of the holiday we occasionally wondered whether we would have a manse to come back to. I can't remember whether we could phone home or not. There was no damage whatsoever to the manse. The abiding memory for all of us was the sudden realisation that our manse had been in the centre of one of the biggest protests that evening.

Rev Jonathan Moxen

* On the Sunday before 12 July each year, the Orange Order holds its "Drumcree parade" in Portadown, when it marches to and from Drumcree Parish Church. It has marched this route since early in the 19th century, when the area was thinly populated. Now, however, most of this march route falls within the town's mainly-Catholic and Nationalist area, which is densely populated.

* The Orange Order is a Protestant organisation based mainly in Northern Ireland and Scotland. It is organised in local groups. Each group is known as a Lodge.

North Antrim Coast

THE MANSE AND THE PRIEST

I had known Michael, the priest, for some time before he came to visit the manse in Dundalk on Thursday 7th September 1989. He wanted to see the North and the manse was handy for that purpose. He also wanted to know if he needed to bring 'civies'! I assured him that whatever he wore it would be OK for his trip north.

I had first met Michael when I worked in the west of Ireland. Before visiting the local school we usually called with the priest as a matter of courtesy. Most visits were short but the visit to Michael was always long as he was full of chat.

On one occasion I tried to give him a hint - I brought a cake along! The cake disappeared into the kitchen. It never reappeared with or without a cup of tea! In his next parish Michael had a housekeeper who usually boiled an egg to go with the cup of tea.

On one occasion Michael asked me to find and read out to him specific verses in the Bible. He told me that the first grace given in baptism was free; with that grace the recipient works to earn more grace. I told him that grace was free from beginning to end. His reply sticks in my mind – "it would be wonderful if that was true."

In 1983 I was asked to give a talk on "Was Martin Luther right?" in a hotel near where Michael lived. When I told him about this he cancelled evening mass and came along.

So it was no surprise that he came along to the manse on 7th September 1989. I collected him from the train station. He intended to stay over the weekend until the following Monday. On Friday and Saturday I took him to two towns in the North – his wish had been fulfilled.

On the Saturday evening Michael informed me that he would be too embarrassed to appear at the service the next day. However, he wanted to hear the Bible being read – the reading was from the book of Ruth. He confessed he had never heard it.

Some time later I was informed that Michael had had a stroke. I was able to visit him in a nursing home. He was feeling sorry for himself and blaming himself for not going to see the doctor earlier. He asked me to give him my blessing. I read the Scriptures with him and prayed. Afterwards he asked for the prayer but I told him that I had used no set form of words. We had a discussion about Jesus being the door and I used the open door of his ward to show that it was a simple thing to walk in through the open door.

Afterwards he phoned me. I asked him about our last discussion. "I am like Zacchaeus," he said. (Those who knew his size could agree!). I further asked him whether he was up or down the tree. He didn't answer.

I was informed of his death some time after the funeral. Our family was glad to have had the opportunity to entertain him in the manse. His own words in the visitor's book are these "Thanks for a lovely few days with you. God Bless."

Rev N.S. Millar

IT'S ONLY A HOUSE

My name is Claire. I love this town. For seventeen of the first eighteen years of my life I lived here. Whenever the opportunity arises I come back to Ballymena, usually to visit my friend Joan who, although she now lives in Dublin, likes to spend part of her vacation and occasional weekends with her parents. I, too, enjoy visiting my parents who are now retired and living about sixty miles away. My other friends have either moved away or else have married local boys and are living in surrounding villages where houses are more affordable. These are the ones who shared my childhood and youth and who were frequent visitors to our house or, to give it its formal title, "The Manse."

The house is on the corner of Old Galgorm Road and Woodland Avenue. I admit that, when I left for University in Manchester, leaving 9 Old Galgorm Road didn't cause me a thought; nor did it when I left it for the last time to return to Glasgow where I now work. From memory I don't even think I looked back as we pulled away from the house.

Perhaps it was because I had been thinking about the house that today I have diverted on to the Old Galgorm Road instead of taking a more direct route home. I slow the car but see nothing: that is because there is nothing to see. I bring the car to a halt, switch off the engine and get out. I go round to the passenger side to avoid the traffic, which grows heavier on this slip road year by year. I put my elbows on the roof of the car and use my hands to cradle my head the better to see what is there. There is nothing.

Emma, my eldest sister, was devastated when she learned that the church committee planned to demolish the Manse.

"*They can't do this to our house!*" she protested.

Of course they could, and they did.

"It's nothing but vandalism!"

She threatened to write in protest to the committee. Dad tried to pour oil on troubled waters by explaining that the house had to be updated and it was probably better to build a new one than try to renovate; anyway, *"it's just a house."* Emma remained unconvinced, even angry.

Sarah, the sister nearest to me in age, is the quiet one, the one who thinks deeply about everything; she seemed to take it in her stride even though I think she regretted the passing of what Emma called *"our house"* – which really wasn't ours, but we knew what she meant. As for me, I was ambivalent. I actually thought Emma had gone a little over the top. Now, however, as I gaze across the road at nothing, I am not so sure.

The Manse was a fun place to live. Although I don't remember, I'm told that our arrival coincided with a change in ownership of a number of the houses in the cul-de-sac, bringing a fresh influx of children, mainly girls. Soon these new arrivals, all seven years old or less, were regular visitors to each other's houses. On Saturdays, however, all paths led to ours. Having negotiated the kitchen, they would then tsunami-like rush the stairs and, one by one, clamber up the ladder into the roof-space, pulling the wooden trap door behind them. Entrance was banned to everyone who failed to present the correct password. In that girl-space a newspaper was compiled and freshly written material broadcast through their "radio station" to the community downstairs and beyond. At first I was excluded, but as the years went on the roof-space became a den for my friends and me too.

The Manse was Dad's workplace. The study was the place where he spent most of his time preparing sermons and talks. While we were not excluded, we knew that this was his den so we allowed him to get on with his work in peace. Our front door must have seen hundreds of couples come through on their way to the drawing room where Dad would take the necessary details for their marriage plans. He was always interested in the body language of these young people, for, although there were plenty of chairs to choose from, they would invariably plump themselves on the settee, seemingly to derive strength from each other. I could never understand why any of them should be nervous in Dad's presence but some, it seems, were. Before the advent of marriage preparation classes he would pass on as much helpful advice as he could, or, at least, I think that is what he did! While we were not privy to what was going on we knew that many other folk came with big problems to discuss.

When we were growing up there were many gatherings held in the Manse. The Church organist came almost every week to plan the Sunday services. Later, when the church became more sophisticated, it was the musical director along with a worship group who appeared. Dad never missed those meetings.

When "small groups" were introduced into the church we were the first to feel the effect, as every other Friday morning just before 7.00 a.m., the sound of cars pulling up and doors banging heralded the arrival of the leaders of these groups. For about one hour they would, according to Dad, "*reflect, plan and pray.*" Usually the front door was left open for them to troop in, and on cold winter mornings they were welcomed by the heat from a fire that had sometimes been lit the night before. Occasionally things didn't go according to plan and dad would have to be wakened by snowballs crashing against the bedroom window. Later he would protest that he had been deep in prayer. I think what those leaders enjoyed most was when they retired to the dining room for breakfast!

Friday, as you night imagine, was a particularly busy morning for Mum who had to make the porridge and the toast. We had to buy an extra big toaster and a second kettle to keep up with demand!

Although Mum was a teacher by profession, the Manse was also her workplace. In it she was not only the manager of the restaurant, but also of the laundrette and the clothes factory; with her wonderful dress-making skills she made most of our clothes. The Manse was also the venue for the various committees she chaired or was involved in. We enjoyed meeting the women of the church and they, in turn, got to know us in our natural habitat.

We entertained quite often, especially on Sundays when visiting preachers would join us for lunch, tea or supper. They came from all over the world, from every continent, including a gentleman from China who was known as the "Miracle Man." The most popular visitors, however, were our grandparents. They came regularly and we loved their company, especially at lunch when Granddad would share his stories and Granny, when she was in the mood, her "nonsense" Irish poems. I also remember the Sunday lunches when we had no visitors and we were on our own. These were special times as we ate, laughed and shared all the funny things that had happened during the week. Lunch would last for hours unless Dad had a funeral to conduct; even then we carried on the chat when he was away.

Then there was the garden, which bordered the house on three sides. The front garden had three large beech trees that provided shade, but which in season shed tons of leaves. We had great fun jumping into these after they had been raked and were waiting to be bagged. When we first arrived our grandparents spent a lot of time working in the garden, trying to get it into shape. They planted shrubs and trees, which grew with us. They built a patio at the side and installed slides and swings at the back that were the envy of the other children in the avenue. The big attraction in the garden, however, was not at the back but at the front: Granddad had climbed one of the trees and fixed a tyre swing to a strong branch. I don't know how an elderly man did that but he did; almost every year afterwards he would regularly climb up to make sure that it remained safe. Granddad loved working in the garden, which was a great relief and help to Dad. A corner of the garden held the last remains of a stray cat, which had became our much loved family pet.

Life in the manse wasn't always sweetness and light. There were dark times too. Emma became seriously ill and we thought she might not recover. Dad and Mum also had severe illnesses. I know there were other things that happened that we never really understood: for example, friends of Mum's would arrive and then, as quickly as they had come, disappear with her into another room. Only later, much later, years later, did we find out that they had come to pray for Dad, perhaps as he chaired a particularly difficult Session or Committee Meeting. We were too young to know about the tensions and difficulties that were in the congregation in those days. I suppose we were protected from much that was not ours to know.

For us the Manse was always a safe place; a place of fun where our friends were always made welcome. Emma and Sarah took this to extremes with their New Year parties: a memorable one had one hundred and twenty-three young people packed into the kitchen, living room and hall! I will never forget the Conga snaking round the house and down the avenue that beautiful night. Not one glass or ornament was broken!

That manse was not pretentious and could be described simply as a family house. It was our family home. Out of the back door three little girls left for their first day at school; out of the front door two beautiful brides passed on their way to their marriage services.

Now there are no squeals of delight, no visitors' footsteps, neither laughter nor tears. The house we loved and grew up in - our secret attic, dad's study, mum's kitchen, and the garden with all its memories - is no more. But the values we learned there: faith in God, love, respect and consideration for others irrespective of race, creed or class are still with us and always will be.

It's cold now. I don't know how long I have been standing here. I wonder if those passing have recognised me as the girl who used to live in the house that once stood so proudly on the corner. I'll go now, just in case someone might recognise me and wonder what is wrong, for the tears are streaming down my cheeks. You were right, Emma, it *was* more than "just a house".

THE PRESBYTERIAN GLADIATOR

An important rule for anybody, particularly a Moderator of the Presbyterian Church in Ireland, is to be on time for any engagement.

To be late can be seen as a slight on those who have invited you. I usually like to be on time, and felt this to be even more important during my year as Moderator, although I admit that sometimes I have been known to sail close to the wind. That is not what happened on a dark and windswept October day in 2002.

My wife and I had left our Ballymena home in plenty of time to reach Greystones, Co. Dublin, where I was to preach the following morning. As the plan was to stay in the manse overnight, we had indicated to the Minister our expected time of arrival.

What did Robert Burns say about "The best laid schemes o' mice and men..."?

The journey was horrendous, with weather and road conditions conspiring to slow us down to almost a crawl. Realising that we were not going to make it in time, we phoned ahead to warn our hosts that there would be a delay. Eventually we arrived at Greystones Manse, full of apologies. Our annoyance was matched only by that of the Minister's six-year-old son who, after ninety minutes' delay, had been able to wait no longer and had impatiently enquired, "Daddy, what time **IS** the Gladiator coming?"

Very Rev Dr. R.I. Birney

ENTERTAINING THE MODERATOR

We, like other manse families, have had the privilege of entertaining many fine people over the years, including some Moderators of the General Assembly. Ronnie Craig was one such; when he and his wife Isobel asked if they could stay in our Newry manse for a night en route to the south of Ireland we were delighted. During his time in office I acted as one of Ronnie's chaplains, so for this reason, and also because I had been his assistant in Carrickfergus, it was important that everything should go well. Everything did go well until breakfast when, gathered around the dining room table, I proposed that I should say grace. "But daddy!" interrupted Emma, our four year old. I indicated that she should wait. Emma, however, was not willing to wait and repeated in a sharper tone this time, "*But Daddy!*" By this time I recognised that, not only was my parental authority being challenged but my credibility as leader in the home was also under threat.

"EMMA!" I said with a certain amount of firmness, even annoyance in my voice, "*please wait until I say grace!*"

At that she struck as quickly as any viper: "But Daddy! We NEVER say grace at breakfast!"

Very Rev Dr. R.I. Birney

NO SIGN OF DRAGONS HERE

Our manse was a fine old house built around the beginning of the twentieth century. It was situated on the Quay Road, which is the main thoroughfare from Ballycastle town centre down to the sea front.

Our family loved living in this large rambling house, and even though it was hard to heat in winter, it was delightfully cool in the summer.

It was a place of many wonderful memories for us as a family. Many a time the house was filled with family and friends, and resounded to the noise of parties for the children as they grew up. It was also a centre for fellowship and significant conversations over a lifetime of ministry. All sorts of people came to visit us for a great many reasons.

One story may serve to illustrate the unexpected side of Manse life!

For a time the house next door to us was a guest house. One summer evening we had all sat up late enjoying good conversation. On the way to bed well after midnight, I went into the study to return something. The window was slightly open and I could hear the unmistakable cry for help coming from the garden next door. I looked out; a couple were standing by the front door of the guest house. I spoke out to them. They had booked in earlier that evening, and, since they said that they were going out to visit friends, had been given a key. When they returned they discovered to their horror that the front door had been snibbed from the inside! The lights were out; no-one was answering their repeated attempts to gain entrance. We tried telephoning, to no avail; in the end we invited the couple to come round for a cup of tea and to stay the night with us. It was the one and only time we have tried to run a guest house! Next morning the couple went next door for breakfast followed by a rapid apology from our neighbours who had gone off to sleep the previous evening hearing neither doorbell nor telephone!

When I was convener of the Overseas Board of the Presbyterian Church in Ireland I often had the job of interviewing prospective candidates for missionary service. In those days the individual, or more often the couple, was sent round a number of board members for informal interview, and often ended up with me. In this way we felt we were able to gain a number of people's impressions of the candidates in preparation for a more formal interview. When such folk arrived Margaret and I would welcome them, trying to set them at their ease. Then Margaret would slip away to prepare something to eat while the candidate and I had our chat together. Inevitably at the end of the evening Margaret would produce the Visitors Book. One delightful couple, who have since spent a lifetime in mission at home and overseas, wrote in the "comments" column the immortal words "No sign of dragons here!" "What does that mean?" Margaret asked.

"Well," they said, "everyone we have met has been so encouraging and so nice that we had made up our minds that you had to be the big bad dragon, and had been kept to the end! But we have really enjoyed ourselves this evening too; we are just relieved there are no dragons here!"

When our children were small, for a few summers we had someone come to help us by keeping an eye on them when we had our duties to carry out. Some of our helpers were students from overseas, and others were CSSM team members or family friends. It was always a time of friendship and fun, as we went off on picnics, outings or visits to other lovely parts of the country. In the evenings we met up with friends often laughing and talking together till a late hour! Not long ago we met up with one of our "summer girls", now an active Church member away from Northern Ireland. We were so thrilled when she reminded us that those weeks were a turning point in her spiritual journey when she had come to know the Lord Jesus in a personal way.

Like many manse families, we had the joy and privilege of having moving and life changing conversations with folk who came from time to time for spiritual help and guidance. Their stories do not belong to us. They are their stories, and it is not for us to tell them. Suffice it to say that every time we pass the old house, now a manse no longer, we give thanks to God for giving us such a happy home there, and for making it also a place that God used to touch so many folk with His grace and Truth.

Very Rev Dr. Godfrey Brown

No Dragons Here

Compilation of Watercolour Pictures from Ireland and Malawi

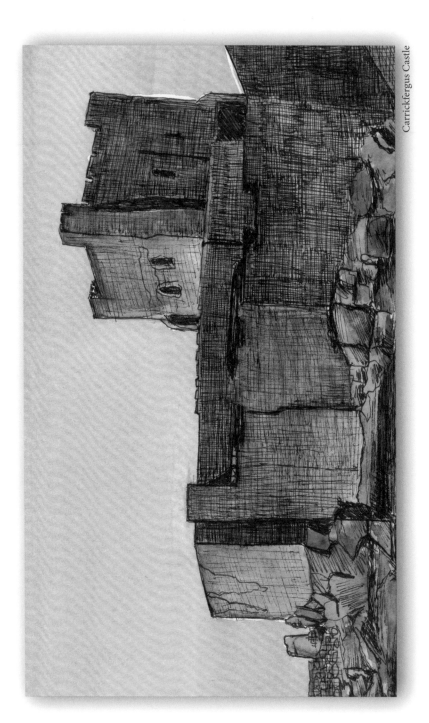

Carrickfergus Castle

White house at Nkhoma

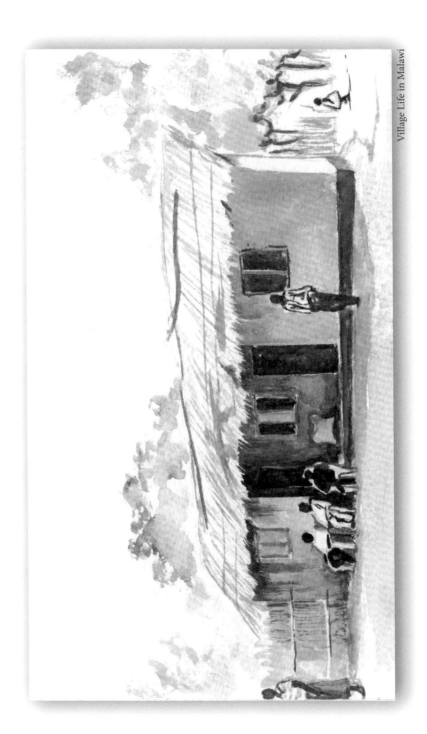

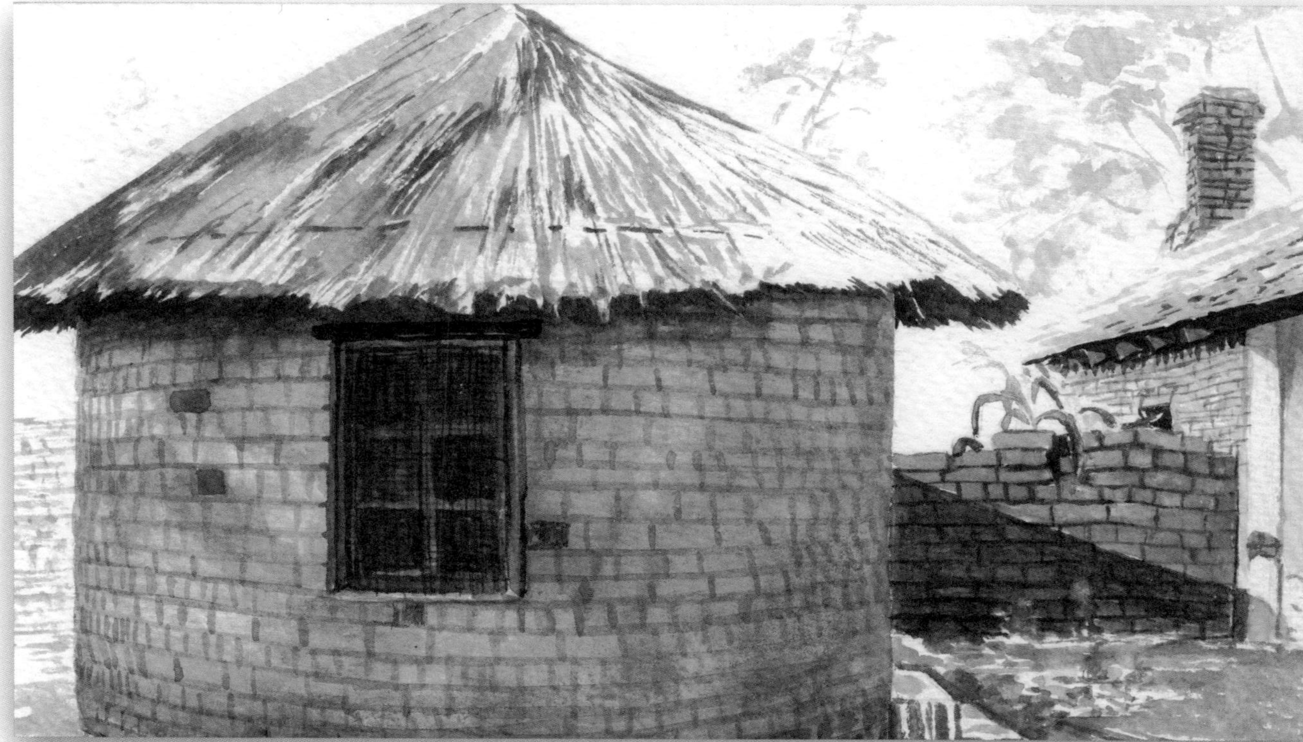

Rondavel at Nkhoma

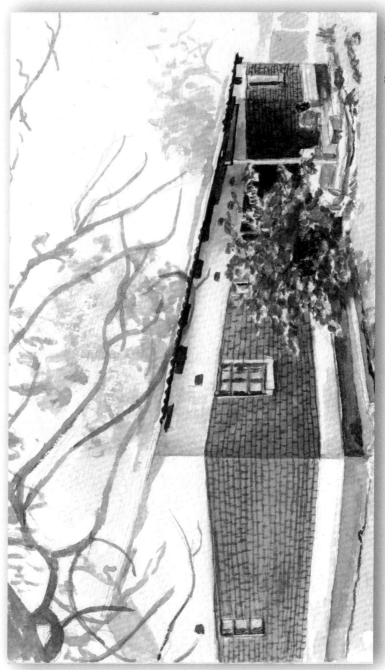

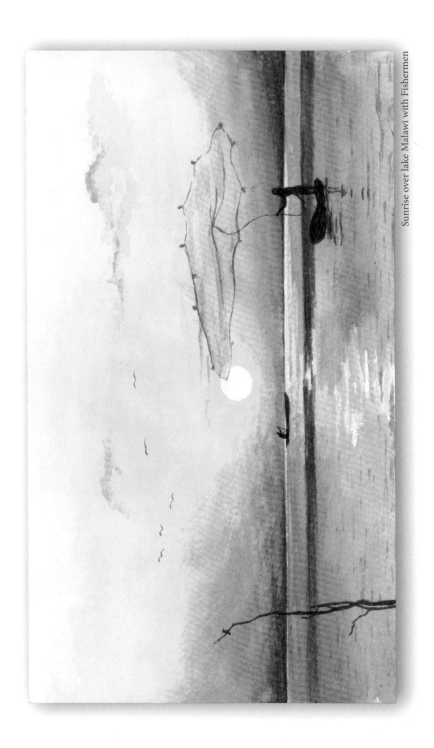

Sunrise over lake Malawi with Fishermen

Map of IRELAND

ATLANTIC
OCEAN

Bushmills
Ballycastle
Coleraine
River
Bann
Londonderry
Ballymena
Larne
Portglenone
Carrickfergus
Donegal
Omagh
Lough
Neagh
Bangor
Lurgan
BELFAST

Sligo

Newry

Dundalk

DUBLIN

Greystones

IRISH
SEA

Cork

0   40 miles

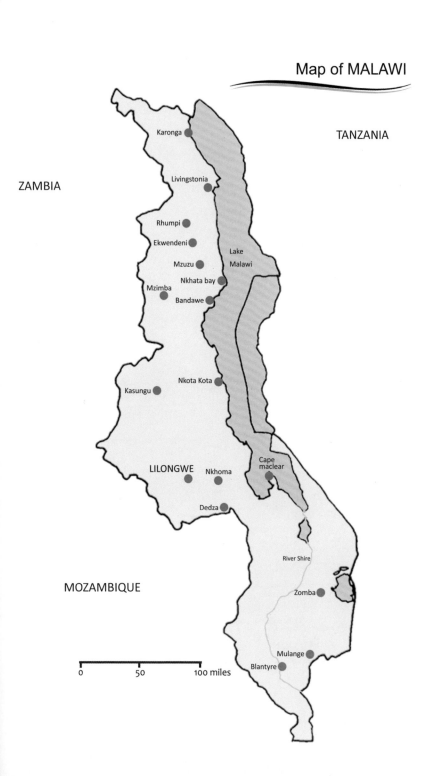

Map of MALAWI

TANZANIA

ZAMBIA

Karonga

Livingstonia

Rhumpi

Ekwendeni

Mzuzu

Lake
Malawi

Nkhata bay

Mzimba

Bandawe

Nkota Kota

Kasungu

LILONGWE   Nkhoma

Cape
maclear

Dedza

River Shire

MOZAMBIQUE

Zomba

Mulange

Blantyre

0   50   100 miles

STORIES FROM MALAWI

Malawi --- who took the name of Jesus there, and who spread the seeds of His Church west of her shimmering ribbon lake?

More than a thousand years after Patrick carried the cross to Ireland we can see far, far away the Portuguese bringing it into Nyasaland*. If we return two or three hundred years later we struggle to find remaining testimony to this, except the name of Maria in a local boat song. But this African story is not finished; there are plenty of pictures still to be drawn.

Casting our glance away from the flurry of manse building in Ireland, we should allow ourselves to travel some six thousand miles to where the Atlantic and Indian oceans meet, and trek north a thousand miles or more. Under the huge, magnificent, hot African sun we will meet somewhere, in the vast wooded expanse, the celebrated Christian explorer, traveller and missionary, David Livingstone. His Scottish heart is burning for Africa and his tales of Lake Nyasa have already lit a spark in the soul of a young Presbyterian theological student, James Stewart. Back in Scotland Stewart sets his face and heart to come to Nyasaland. Later if we wait by the banks of the mighty Zambezi we can feel his excitement as that young brave heart meets Livingstone. As we dare to share his northward journey towards the lake it slowly dawns on us that there will be no happy ending to this adventure: two and a half years later as we join Stewart's waiting, wondering friends we are compelled to witness his sad homecoming: penniless, full of fever, and near to death. Inside many a whitewashed cottage are breathed those cruel words : "we told you so." We can feel Stewart's pain when he is refused permission to return to the lake; we can admire his courage when he takes up the challenge of going instead to Lovedale in South Africa and we can feel confident of hearing more about this young man.

*Nyasaland is the former name for Malawi

If we could go where Stewart could not, we would find Living-stone again, gazing still on the stunning sapphire waters of Lake Nyasa, with the hills of Tanzania hazy in the distance; as we stand beside him he will surely tell us of his enduring hope that some day the gospel will be written on the walls of the thousands of lakeshore huts and on the hearts of their people. Watching still, we glimpse that tenacious man forcing a way up the sloping wooded hills and deep into the central regions, where he will keep trekking for seven years, will see scenes too terrible to be drawn on any wall, and die at Ilala in the continent that had long ago captured his heart.

Following Livingstone's body back to England in 1874, we again meet Dr James Stewart: as he stands at Livingstone's open grave in Westminster Abbey, the smouldering in his heart for Nyasaland bursts into a fierce blaze, a passion which drives him to talk, pray and influence others - until we see a group of men from Scottish Presbyterian churches with one Anglican and one Baptist uniting to plan Christian work in Africa.

At the West India Docks in London on 21st May 1875 we can sense the excitement as the "Walmer Castle" is loaded with provisions and supplies for two years, yards of calico for barter and, intriguingly, a dismantled steamer called the Ilala.

Going aboard we join the men of the Livingstonia Expedition. The second in command is no seaman but a twenty four year old medical doctor and ordained preacher from Aberdeen called Robert Laws. His heart and mind and soul can still clearly recall the vivid picture of himself as a very young child praying that God would send him to Africa.

On June 26th in Cape Town, along with an assortment of Africans hired for boat duties, cooking, interpreting, and the like, we all board another vessel – a German schooner hired for the trip up the east coast of Africa. After twenty-five days sailing, the steamy, malaria-infested Zambezi delta appears through the heat haze. We come ashore. In the following days we see trees being felled, men's bodies wracked with fever and sickness, people building and bartering. And we see Laws, with little gatherings around him, explaining the message of Jesus.

Then, on Tuesday August 10th, the re-assembled Ilala, every carefully polished screw in place, takes us on her inland river voyage. For two months, such scenes as we could barely imagine to be true meet us --- herds of elephants and antelope feeding in the distance, crocodiles and hippos lurking in the water, lions and leopards prowling by night, and always, always the clouds of insatiable mosquitoes. We meet a chief with 40 wives, slave traders with white robes and guns; we feel scorching heat, hear lashing rain and see thunderstorms beyond our experience and the incredible sight of 200 Africans carrying the Ilala piece by precious piece over a staggering seventy miles where the river is impassable.

Then one morning in the second week of October, as the sun rises over the mountain-tops, the Ilala glides into the glorious liquid gold of Lake Nyasa. Gathering his crew, Laws goes ashore at Cape Maclear on the southern tip of the lake. If we stay to see them courageously realising their calling and vision, we must be ready to share the pain, frustration and adventure of surviving lake storms, relentless malarial fever, and befriending tribal chiefs. Finally we can see the last few sticks being lashed together and the last bundles of thatch tied into place: the very first Presbyterian manse is erected in Nyasaland.

Stories were beginning in other corners too: if we journey southwards for a day and a half down the valley of the River Shire, past the massive Zomba plateau and into the Shire highlands, we will come to the Blantyre mission station where we will find another manse of poles and grass built by the established Church of Scotland missionaries in 1876. We might linger there before taking time, on the trek back up to Maclear, to make a detour northwards and arrive at a place called Mvera. Listening to a group of workers from the Dutch Reformed Church, we catch the unmistakable North Antrim accent of young Samuel McClure from Cloughmills. Not many months later, if we enter any of the manses he had built at Mvera, Nkhoma or Kongwe we would here the story of McClure lying ill of blackwater fever. The final picture would be of his body being buried among the trees of a shady grove in Nkhoma.

Back at Cape Maclear we can rejoin Dr Laws. There comes a morning when he and his party leave five years' hard labour and five European graves behind them; we dare to travel up north with them to a place called Bandawe on the western shores of Lake Nyasa, set between the sands and the forested mountains. It is home to the Ngoni Tribe. We have not come here to rest or relax, because the persistent, relentless work continues and more stories will be written. Buildings of timber, mud and thatch go up: among them a manse. On their walls could be written the stories of those days – stories of tribal warfare, long periods of fever, confrontations with slave caravans where men were chained neck to neck; stories of lions, white ants and jiggers; and stories of the work moving slowly, slowly forward.

Thirteen years later, if our bodies have enough vigour and our hearts enough valour, we must move on with Dr Laws, his wife, a few Tonga workers, and the carpenter, as they leave Bandawe to the care of others and head out into yet more unknown territory. The Ilala carries us north up the western side of the lake, until at last the steeply sloping sides of Mount Waller come into view and near it the Kondowe plateau. We have to continue on foot; in the scorching heat we start to climb the treacherous sides of the plateau, stumbling over rocky ground and fighting through thick jungle. Far below, the dazzling white foam meets golden sands as the cool water of the lake breaks ashore. As we pass the thundering waterfalls at Manchewe we can spot tribal folks living in caves; all round the hillside there are small round dwellings. At almost 3,000 feet above sea level we find ourselves on a small plateau about a mile square. Behind us mountains tower far up into the clouds. With its cooler, crisper climate this seems the perfect site to establish a mission, so the usual back-breaking tasks of tree felling, brick making, planting and building begins all over again, continuing daily from dawn to dusk. The place is named Livingstonia. If we could remain here long enough we would see amazing stories being written: schools are built, with a dream that some day there will be a university here; a carpentry shop and a printing press are set up; an electricity power station is constructed; water is made to run up the hill; a hospital is erected; here and there little groups are meeting to study God's Word or pray. Lives are being changed by God's love. We would finally see a church being built from red baked bricks, and through the trees on the very edge of the plateau, looking away to the lake and the hills of Tanzania, is the manse, built of grey, quarried stone, with a roof of corrugated iron. For the next 64 years we can watch and listen as God allows the story of the Presbyterian Church in Nyasaland to be written. Then, in 1958, the Irish chapter begins.

In 1957 the growing Presbyterian Church in Malawi issued a plea for help to the Presbyterian church in Ireland. The following year a son of the manse, Rev Bill Jackson, his wife Dorothy and their two children packed their belongings and left Ireland for Africa.

Let's travel with them that long journey to Karonga on the northern tip of Lake Malawi. What a delight to join Mr Jackson as he enters for the first time the manse of Rev Andrew Kayira at Karonga Old Mission Station. Under the big mango tree by the lakeshore, we sense a firm friendship being forged between the two men in the cool interior of that mud brick, roughly thatched manse. Over the following months many a story unfolds of shared journeys by bicycle and on foot to far flung hill villages; stories of sermons preached, tea drunk and meals of nsima and relish shared. As we eventually climb with Jackson up that Kondowe escarpment again, to his temporary residence at Livingstonia: what a surprise! Four hundred and fifty people now live here; that old stone manse is now the council offices.

As the months pass a grumbling uneasiness in the country breaks into civil unrest. Some ministers, whose faith does not allow them to undersign the political demands of Congress, are being targeted. Through the small unglazed windows of manses at Rhumpi, Mventite and Karonga we can see ugly scenes of angry crowds with spears; we hear mocking and abuse. Yet the men inside, trusting in God, sleep peacefully with their families, or step outside to speak of calmness and patience.

Finally it is safe to travel again. We see charred remains of manse walls at Karonga and Deep Bay. They tell dark stories of people angry with ministers who had tried to build peace, but also stories bright with the unquenchable courage and faithfulness of those men. If we stay awhile by the lake at Karonga we can watch two new manses with cool khondis and smart corrugated iron roofs rising from the ashes – one for Bill Jackson and one for Andrew Kayira.

Along that pathway opened up from Ireland to Malawi others came to share in the work of the Church. If we travel the five hundred miles to the south and stop one Sunday in April at Blantyre manse there are three small European boys playing – all sons of missionaries. We can see one of them, young Martin Lewis, on the roof. Later we hear the heartbreaking story of how he became entangled on the electrical wires and died, marking those manse walls with anguish and heartache. Not far away we are invited into the home of a Malawian minister: a manse whose thatch was leaking so badly in the rainy season that his young boy died of pneumonia. Within those low mud walls, in the dimness, we can feel the sorrow.

Over the years stories of sadness, joy, excitement, turmoil and fun have been written inside Malawian manses. Come on a journey, enjoy the pictures and have your heart warmed by the stories.

Shore of Lake Malawi

TWO TALES FROM THE WHITE HOUSE

There are two possible reasons why The White House is so called: it is the only house at Nkhoma Mission Station which is painted white, and it was built for two white lady missionaries.

It is believed that the White House was built by Mr Samuel McClure from Cloughmills, N.Ireland, who was the carpenter and builder for the mission between 1897 and 1901. Mr McClure helped to build the churches at Mvera and Nkhoma, but sadly later contracted blackwater fever, died and was buried at Nkhoma. His grave and headstone can be seen in a shady tree lined glade at Nkhoma mission station.

THE BLIND MAN

A blind man often came to the house to look for lodgings. We allowed him to stay in the rondavel, specially built for guests, at the back of the manse. Sometimes he would bring his wife and three children with him to stay. On one occasion he stayed for three months.

We could not say to him, "When are you going?" This would have been rude.

One day he asked my wife and me, "Do other people come here for help? If it is so, do not give them anything. I am the only one you should help."

I replied that what we have is from the Lord and we will share it with whoever asks, if we are able. The blind man was not pleased with that answer and went away. We never saw him again.

THE PREACHER

One day a young man came to our door. He did not introduce himself but only said, "God has sent me to preach here."

I asked, "How do you know that?" to which he replied, "Because He says I must preach."

My response was that the Lord had not told me about this.

The young man, who had come up from Blantyre, was very insistent and told me, "If you refuse, you might have big problems because the Lord is telling me NOW to preach here."

I explained that it would be impossible for him to stay and preach in the area because down in the village there was cholera – people were dying like flies. If he stayed or went into the village at all he might catch cholera and die a terrible death. However, I did invite the young man to stay for the night rather than travel the long distance south to Blantyre that day.

The young man very quickly refused my offer with the remark, "I think I have not heard the Lord well!"

With that he turned and went away.

I never saw him again.

Rev K.J. Mgawi

Shore of Lake Malawi

THE MOVE

Bwiba manse in the Karonga district was built in the 1970's. Rev Andrew Kayira, who studied at Union College in Belfast and was assistant for a short time in Gt. Victoria Street Church, lived in Bwiba Manse for 27 years of his ministry.

After being allocated to Bwiba congregation I moved to this manse with my wife and family on 19th November 2008. We were very excited – many well known ministers had lived here - we knew there was a great history to this place. Changes had been made to the manse building; extensions had been built. There was no water supply inside the old building so when the new rooms were added the toilet and bathroom had to be placed down at one end of the house where water pipes could easily be installed.

At Bwiba, like many other manses, all cooking for the congregation affairs is done by the Umanyano at the manse. The cooking equipment is kept in a store at the manse. All keys for the church are also kept here so the watchman comes every morning and evening to collect or return the keys. It is the job of the minister to monitor where the watchman is.

The day I moved here with my family we came in the Synod lorry. We had started packing; we were leaving the manse at 6.00 a.m. In the lorry were all our belongings, including furniture, our 10 children, ages ranging from 8 to 28, two sisters of mine and two men from our previous congregation who were helping us with the move. We arrived here at 3.00 p.m. It was very hot. Women from Bwiba church were here waiting to welcome us and also to escort away the minister who was leaving Bwiba. The Umanyano had prepared some food for us - rice, nsima and beef.

We began to take everything off the lorry to allow the other minister and his family to pack their belongings. We started to carry the whole lot into the manse, but discovered that our sofa and chest would not fit through the door. They had to be left outside all night making us very afraid that someone would come during the night and take them away. It was dark by the time we got into the manse. There are four bedrooms in this manse, one food store and one other store room. For some reason the sleeping was difficult.

Next morning the carpenters came and took off the door to allow us to bring the sofa and chest indoors.

In the first few days after that our children began to ask questions. "Is this where we have come to?" "Why are there so many mosquitoes here?" "Why is it so hot here?" "Why do we have to come here?"

Four days after our arrival the water board closed off the water. Three days later we held a session meeting to try to think of some way to resolve the situation. My wife and daughters walked for about 4 kilometres to collect water. It felt very good when eventually the water was turned back on.

Moving is never easy but we have to work wherever the church sends us.

Rev Norman Hara

Shore of Lake Malawi

YOU WILL CERTAINLY DIE THIS NIGHT

In the late 1950's, Karonga was in turmoil; the African National Congress was active in the area, and Rev Andrew Kayira was being severely threatened because he was friendly with Europeans.

The following incident from that time is included in "Send us Friends" by Bill Jackson, as it was told to him by Andrew:

I heard that a mob had gathered, and they shouted that I should be killed that night. They knew that I had refused to take a Congress card, but now they were chiefly angry because, following our preaching programme, I had allowed the DC to preach at the Church the previous Sunday.

One of my elders, Wilson Kyumba, had been at this meeting of the mob. That night Wilson Kyumba came to the manse. Only three elders came to the manse during this time. All the elders had been threatened that they would suffer severely themselves if they came near me. Mr Kyumba told me what he had heard at the meeting of the mob that day and he said to me, "I have not come to tell you to leave home; but I've come to say that you must stay here at the manse. This is your place. God will protect you and help you!"

After he had gone, I went and prayed alone. I was afraid. Then I called my wife and family, and prayed with them. I told my wife our position, and then said, "We must stay!" She agreed.

No one came that night.

The next evening some teachers came to see me.

"It is only by chance that you have slept this past night," they said, and they pleaded with me, "You must leave!"

"God has put me here," I replied, "This is my place and I cannot leave."

They stayed a long time trying to persuade me. "This is not

courage at all," they said. Finally, when they saw that I could not be moved, they said, "Let us take your wife and children away to safety."

"Go and see her for yourselves," I replied, "and if she is willing, take her with you." My wife refused to leave me.

They went away then, sorrowfully, and slowly. I was not sad, however, for I felt that death was not near. I knew God was there.

Later that night, two women came. When they saw me, they began to weep.

"You are still alive!" they cried. They were very surprised. "God is very powerful! But now you must please, please leave this place!"

"Let us trust God," I answered.

"But they tell us you will certainly die this night!"

Rev Jackson goes on:

The following afternoon, Andrew told me how he had been sitting outside in his deck chair reading, when some schoolboys had come to the big mango tree which stood about 150 yards from his front door. As I have mentioned, primary schoolboys could be late teenagers, big fellows. They began to shout abuse and to mock him. He felt very afraid, but he ignored them. And then, as they began to leave, quite unexpectedly, a great sense of joy welled up inside him, and he thought of Jesus' words:

"Blessed are you when men revile you and persecute you and utter all kinds of evil against you falsely on my account. Rejoice and be glad, for your reward is great in heaven, for so men persecuted the prophets who were before you."

"Afterwards," he said, "I heard that people had come on two separate nights to burn the manse. The first time, after discussion nearby, they changed their minds and went back. The second time, they saw my torch as I walked unwittingly towards them in the darkness, and since they had wanted to set fire to the manse while I was asleep inside, they went away."

LIFE IN MZUZU MANSE

The word Mzuzu in Tumbuka language derives from the original word for wild bananas which are called Vizuza or Chizuza: these bananas are not edible. The white missionaries failed to pronounce the word correctly and pronounced it as Mzuzu which has remained the name of the city to his day. Mzuzu congregation was at first a vestry or prayer house under Ekwendeni parish, but as a result of church growth Mzuzu became a congregation and in about 1945 the Mzuzu Manse was erected. The congregation is also known as St Andrew's congregation.

Mzuzu Manse is well known in the city as a Samaritan House, where all kinds of people with many health and spiritual problems come. These visitors come almost every day, forcing the church session to budget for it every year. Some come just to demand food at early hours of the morning; some will demand certain types of food; some will ask to use your plates; some enter without knocking, go straight to the kitchen and pick up any food that is available that day. When I first occupied the manse it was somehow trying because in other manses where I had lived there would be such callers, but not daily!

Sometimes we are tempted to ask questions: "Why do these people come to the manse daily?" but now we have come to know that it is God's grace doing His work. As well as the unannounced visitors, we have morning and evening prayers, special church meetings, Bible studies, meetings to arrange funerals; we must also have a supply of Bibles and Hymn Books on our shelves for the needy.

Staying in Mzuzu Manse has helped my wife, Ruth, and me to understand better the role of the manse in the African community context. We have seen that the manse must be a place where needy people can come for food and shelter; where spiritual seekers can find answers; where the manse family knows the home does not belong to them but to all; where there is no need of publicity in order for it to be known that, here, God's grace is free to all. It is to be a light in the community.

In this manse the occupants must be strong, genuine Christians, otherwise they may run and leave! To stay you must know that God has called you to be His servant not the boss!

Rev Levi Nyondo

Shore of Lake Malawi

DISCONNECTION AT MZUZU MANSE

The years 1992 and 1993 brought political change to Malawi as the country moved from one party rule to multiplicity. This change affected Mzuzu.

The minister in Mzuzu Manse was involved in the political struggle for change, supporting AFORD: Alliance for Democracy, an anti-government pressure group. The party had no office and its leader was in detention. Mzuzu Manse acted as a centre of communication for pressure group members. The manse telephone was being used for communication purposes. Government believed that some political documents were distributed through the manse. The minister of the church was put in detention and the manse was to be searched by government intelligence.

There was sadness around the manse lest all the Christians should be termed as government opponents. On the other hand, some Christians were suspected as betrayers of the manse.

Non-Christians who were advocating for political change visited the manse frequently. By 1994 the manse telephone had accumulated a bill of MK34,000 which was too much for the church to pay. The Alliance for Democracy failed to assist the church to clear this bill. The result was disconnection of the line. The manse then had no means of telephone communication until, eventually, the church applied for a new line in sympathy for their minister.

Mr Aupson W. Thole

THERE WAS LIGHTNING

On 22nd November 1984 the son of a minister died. The funeral was at Emanyeleni Mombwe congregation. I was informed because at that time I was Presbytery clerk of Ekwendeni and Bandawe Presbytery. I set off from Mzuzu with my wife, Mama Mliska Chavula and two members of the women's guild. When we arrived everything was ready, just waiting for myself and Mama Mliska.

It was 10.30 a.m. I conducted the service. There were about 1,500 people present. The deceased was to be buried 100 meters from the manse. The General Secretary of Livingstonia Synod, Rev W.P. Chibambo, came while the service was going on and stayed until the service was over. When the service finished it was showery - some people ran away to shelter; some, including Mama Mliska Chavula, the two members of the women's guild who had accompanied us and Rev E.F. Jere went into the church building. There was lightning. After about three minutes a big, loud crack of lightning came. My wife, the members of the women's guild, the Rev E.F. Jere and others ran into the church and sat in the pulpit. The loud crack of lightning hit my wife as she sat in the pulpit. I was sheltering in a small house outside; a man came to tell me that three people including my wife had been affected by the lightning. I ran into the church straight away. The General Secretary came as well; we saw Rev Jere lying down, and a woman who was very badly affected. I did not recognise the woman to be my wife. We carried the lady in the vehicle of the General Secretary to Rhumpi. I still did not know it was my wife. We waited 30 minutes, not knowing what was happening. After 35 minutes the Doctor came.

The Dr. asked, "Are you Rev M.Z. Chavula? Did you come with a woman?"

I answered, "Yes."

The Dr. said, "The woman is dead."

I said, "What?"

Someone told the doctor not to tell me yet it was my wife. After ten minutes the General Secretary and the doctor came to me; they prayed. The General Secretary told me to stay cool. Then the doctor said to me, "Because you are a minister this will not shake you, but let me tell you to-day your beloved wife has been taken into God's hands."

Then I said, "Just tell me – is my wife dead?"

"Yes", said the doctor.

I felt a big crack.

After 30 minutes I asked, "Can I go and see her?"

The doctor said, "No, just wait."

After some time the doctor said, "Come."

I went with the General Secretary and the doctor to see her in the hospital. It was 3.00 p.m. I stayed there in the hospital till 6.00 p.m. The General Secretary telephoned Mzuzu to let them know what had happened.

At 8.00 p.m. we carried my wife from Rhumpi to Mzuzu; many members had been told and were there to welcome us into the manse. There was a mortuary at St. John's hospital, but no fridge. The congregation thought we could find a box the next day.

Next day I could not believe it had happened. I had a son of six years old, Benjamin. We were taking the dead body to Enyezini.

Next day many Christians came for the burial. There was an Umanyano choir. Many choirs.

Some members from the Catholic Church also joined. The funeral took place. I stayed at home for three days.

When I went back to Mzuzu many Christians were waiting for us at the manse. This is when I began to think about my wife. I thought: "She is no longer here." I could not sleep. It took me about a month to sleep.

After about a year some people came from my late wife's village.

They asked me, "How are you going to look after your son? Will you give him to us to look after?"

I said, "No."

After a week they came again. "To-day we would like to ask you if one of the younger sisters of your late wife can look after your son."

I called my parents for advice.

They told me, "If they are willing and if you are also willing, if one can take care of your son we will give the O.K."

The next day they came again from my wife's village. "We are only worried about your son, so we have come with an idea: if you want you can talk to Dora and Josephine."

Dora was the older sister and Josephine younger. By then Dora was a nurse at St. John's hospital; Josephine was at Ekwendeni Nursing School. It took me three weeks. Then I called Dora. We discussed and she said, "Let me think about it."

Two days later the women came. "Have you discussed?"

I told them that I had talked to Dora. The same day she came, we discussed again.

She said, "I can take care of Benjamin."

That was the end of my discussion with Dora. We sent word to relatives.

The relatives said to Dora, "Now you will be the minister's wife."

It was announced in Mzuzu congregation. After this we went home for official wedding of myself and Dora. Since then Dora and I have had three children.

In short this is how it happened.

Some ministers came to offer condolences in my sorrow.

I have known much sorrow but I know the truth that God is with me through pain and sorrow and I want to thank Him for that.

Rev M. Z. Chavula

SOME THOUGHTS ON MANSE LIFE IN 2007

A minister of the Word and sacrament needs a good accommodation from where he can perform spiritual duties for the people to whom he is called. The accommodation should be rent free because, despite being a graduate, the minister is given a stipend (a contribution for living allowances from the congregation), not a salary. At present the starting stipend is 8,000MK.

For the accommodation, the congregation are expected to supply furniture, mattresses, bedding, cooking utensils. The congregation employs a house mother who is responsible for welcoming visitors when the Mama Mliska is away, as well as working at the house to help Mama Mliska.

The manse should be big enough so as to offer the following accommodation: bedroom for the minister, a room for the boys, a room for the girls, a room for female guests, a room for male guests, dining room, sitting room and a store room. There must be a kitchen (this will be outside) with some boys' quarters including a bathroom. The congregation should also provide firewood used to cook food because very few manses in Malawi have got cookers.

The whole purpose of the above is for welcoming guests from within or without the congregation. The manse is used as a guest house. It should be ready to welcome guests at any time during day hours or night hours.

The manse family should live in harmony and peacefully. To live exemplary lives is one way of propagating the Gospel through the minister, however as human beings, problems do not fail to come to us! From what I have experienced, there are sorrows, problems in the congregation or some earthly temptations. In all situations the minister must be on his knees praying to God for help. I have concrete examples where God's hand toughened us when we were surrounded by critical problems. We should not lose hope: God is at our disposal to rescue us from all dangers.

A NIGHT TIME ATTACK

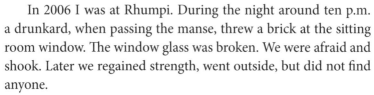

In 2006 I was at Rhumpi. During the night around ten p.m. a drunkard, when passing the manse, threw a brick at the sitting room window. The window glass was broken. We were afraid and shook. Later we regained strength, went outside, but did not find anyone.

In the morning we summoned an emergency session meeting to discuss the issue. This forum did not help. Instead we just prayed to God to replace the broken windows. God answered in a way we were not expecting. The drunkard got mad and came himself to the manse, confessing, while literally naked.

From this scenario, I learned that when we pray, we should not curse anyone.

Rev W.H. Beza

Shore of Lake Malawi

THE MAN WHO ATE A SNAKE

There was a man called Ngulukie who used to come to visit me at Kamanga Manse, in the Rhumpi Presbytery, around midnight. He always asked me to pray for him. The man was a church goer but he had many problems.

Nkulukie became totally mad from smoking Indian hemp for a long time. He would go around looking rejected, eating from rubbish bins. He became homeless and violent.

Nkulukie, because he was mad, came to believe that he was God and gave himself the name of Jesus. He would do piece work for short periods of time but was not able to keep a job for long. It was strange that he still came to the manse to ask me to pray for him even though he believed that he himself was Jesus. I always prayed for him.

Now there was a beer tent about 100 metres from the local school which upset the church members because it was a very bad influence on the community, especially the school children. Every effort to have the beer tent closed was of no effect. Because Nkulukie believed he was Jesus he said he was unhappy to see people drinking in the community; one day he burned to ashes the beer tent. Even though Nkulukie was a nuisance in the area, many of the people were happy to see the end of the beer tent – the Church was pleased that it was gone!

A week later when Nkulukie was out walking he met a snake. It would not be uncommon to see snakes while walking out in the countryside. Because he thought he was Jesus, Nkulukie saw the snake to be Lucifer. He beat the snake heavily with his walking stick, killing it. He then began to eat the snake, starting at its head.

Two days later Nkulukie died of snake poisoning.

Rev Daniel Chaomba

A BOY FROM MPAMBA

In January 2007 our first born boy by the name Andrew was selected to go to Livingstonia Secondary School to start his form one (Secondary School Education). After three weeks at the school he started experiencing some changes in spiritual life. On a certain night after coming back from the evening studies just near to the boys' hostels where he was residing, two girls were standing together in the semi-darkness of the hostels, whispering in hushed voices. What was it that made these girls so different from the others?

He had noticed them before. They were always together, never making friends with anyone else. A strange bond held them together. In fact, he never saw them apart. No-one seemed to know very much about them.

Yes, there was something different about them – something eerie and strange. Curiosity was his constant companion and he decided to investigate. Since the hostels were always in semi-darkness it wasn't difficult to creep up behind them and listen. Standing in the shadowy doorway of the bathing room, he listened carefully to the two whispering girls.

Although he was unable to hear much that was said, he heard something about the Satanists' temple. He held his breath. It was impossible to hear more. If he wanted to hear what they were saying, he would have to disclose his presence. He stepped out from the shadows and said brightly, "What's all this about the Satanists' temple?"

The two girls were startled. "We can't tell you anything about it. It's a secret."

"I gathered that," he sniffed, "but I would like to know."

The two girls probably thought he had overheard the entire

conversation. They looked at one another, and then one of them said, "If you promise never to say anything to anyone about it . . ."

He agreed not to say a word.

"We are Satanists and worship at the temple of Satan."

"Can I come too?"

They again exchanged glances and then agreed.

"Be outside this hostel at eleven o'clock tomorrow, and we'll take you."

On the next evening he stood with bated breath at the appointed place. At eleven o'clock sharp a large black car drew up. The two girls were seated in the back. The driver instructed Andrew to get inside.

"You will have to wear a blindfold, as this is the first time for you. No one must know where the temple is situated." He had no objection. Indeed, the blindfold only added to the excitement. His heart was beating very fast. The journey was soon over. He was led up a short flight of steps, and the blindfold was removed.

What he saw was astonishing and very mysterious. He was standing at the back of a very large hall, filled with about five hundred people. A platform at the front was draped in black. On a throne-like seat sat a robed and hooded figure. His garments were embroidered with snakes, dragons, and flames of fire. Around him in a semi-circle stood some thirteen figures, also robed in black.

His first impulse as he took in the scene was to giggle, but because of the serious expression of the people he restrained himself. It was just as well that he did, for he had placed himself in a hazardous situation. The figures around the platform were the priests and priestesses of the order of Satanism. His next impulse was to run away as far as he could, but he seemed to be glued to the spot.

The ceremony began. Priests and priestesses chanted in a strange rhythmic chant that grew louder and louder as the robed figure in the centre stepped down from the platform. Two of the priests removed his hood, and everyone bowed down and worshipped him, falling prostrate on the ground. He was just an observer, of course, and remained standing. "That's the chief

Satanist," one of the girls with him explained. "He must be obeyed at all times."

Unable to speak, Andrew merely nodded and continued to watch in fascination. "He represents Satan on the earth," said the girl, her voice trembling in awe. Little did he realise that he had walked into the most ancient order of Satanism in the world. "Watch, and listen carefully," said the girl again. "I will explain as the ceremony proceeds."

The whole congregation was now chanting prayers to the chief Satanist in that same strange rhythmic way. Everyone's eyes were on him. Priests and priestesses waited upon him as he kissed the vessels, the knives and the emblem of Satanists that had been taken from the high altar.

"He is dedicating the temple and the vessels to Lucifer."

Suddenly the dim lights went out, and flaming torches were lit. For the first time he saw the effigies of Satan around the walls. They seemed to come alive as the ceremony continued.

A white cockerel was brought in, and its neck was wrung right on the steps that led to the throne and altar. Blood was everywhere. Then the cockerel was offered to Satan in sacrifice with more chants and prayers. Everything was done in the name of Satan, "Diablos," and everyone was excited and in deadly earnest. He was surprised to find the chief Satanist looking right at him. It seemed as if his eyes were piercing right through him. He shivered.

The whole ceremony lasted some two hours. It had been an awesome, yet evil, experience. The chief Satanist appeared at the back of the hall in street attire, and he came over to him. "Do you want to join us?" he asked.

"I don't know. I was a bit frightened by it all."

"There's no need for fear," he smiled. Andrew could not help noticing the admiring glances he was giving him. "I hope to see you again at the meeting," he said and disappeared.

After encountering all these, our son, Andrew, got sick after revealing to friends what he had seen the previous night. Then the headmaster of Livingstonia Secondary School sent our boy,

Andrew, home to Mpamba CCAP Manse where I was residing before I was transferred to Zolozolo Church in Mzuzu.

Our thirteen year old boy Andrew started revealing to his Mum what he had come across whilst he was at school. Because he had revealed what had happened, the power from the darkness attacked Andrew greatly so that one day he was nearly dying after a kitchen had collapsed on him. Fortunately he was rushed to Ekwendeni Mission Hospital for body examination and treatment. He led a miserable life due to fear of Satanism. In Mpamba Manse, before the accident he encountered something strange in the night: a voice in darkness came to him, whilst he was half way sleeping in the manse, which said, "You can't run away from us, we have followed you. If you don't abide by the regulations you will die."

This manse in which we had been living had been existing for almost ten years up to the time when the powers from the darkness wanted to get rid of the life of our son Andrew.

God has given us a strong weapon to get rid of all things in the darkness, a prayer. "For I am persuaded that neither death nor life nor angels nor principalities nor powers nor things present nor things to come nor height nor depth nor any other creature shall be able to separate us from the love of God, which is in Christ Jesus, our Lord." "Nor witch nor Satanist," I added. No, nothing can separate our family from Jesus or the truth.

Our Jesus was stronger than any witch or Satanist. The Lord Jesus Himself dealt with the witches that threatened our son. No harm can come to Andrew. The hand of God has been protecting him every hour up to this day.

Rev Rodgers V. Banda

THREE SHORT STORIES FROM PHIRI

Phiri Manse is situated about I mile from the Chintheche turn off on the Mzuzu to Nkhatabay Road. The manse was first built in 1928 from grass and poles.

A YOUNG MAN

Manses are sometimes nicknamed guesthouses or rest houses. All the time visitors are at the manse with and without appointments. Church elders and local leaders sometimes send the stranded people to seek a place for a night of refuge at the manse.

One day in January 2007 a young man came to the manse at Phiri at 7.00 p.m. saying he had been sent by the village headman. This young visitor wanted a place to spend a night for he had no relations in the area. Surprisingly, when morning came, he didn't leave and was in the manse for two more days.

Rev I. M. Malongo

A MIRACLE

In December 2007 when we arrived to live at Phiri Manse with our family, we brought with us some bags of maize. We had to support a wide family circle – my family and my wife Diane's family. Soon the maize was almost all gone. There was only a small piece of planting land round the manse. People round here ate cassava nsima which is different to where we had come from where they eat maize nsima. Our children could not eat the cassava nsima. One day our last meal was cooked.

My wife asked me, "What will we do tomorrow? This is my last flour."

Together we decided that tomorrow we would not ask the elders for flour.

That evening a visitor called from Chinteche. We did not know the man; he brought with him no certificate of identity from another church. We did not know if he could be a thief and a robber. Visitors from other churches should bring a certificate of identification when they come looking for help, uninvited, to a manse.

We had two problems which gave us a headache. We had a problem of security because we did not know this man and also we had no extra food to offer him. I called an elder from Chinteche to identify our visitor, but he could not.

The visitor shared our last meal.

The following morning, early, some elders from our congregation came to visit. They brought with them a bag of maize.

My wife and I said, "God is able to provide for us."

It was just like the story in the Bible where the widow shared her last meal with Elijah and God provided her with more meal and oil.

Rev Joseph Chimembe

TWO MAD MEN

It was in July 2006 when two mad men arrived at the manse at respective times. I and my wife realised that these men were after food. When the food was made ready the mistake we made was that both of them were given the food on the same plate. We were surprised to see and hear that the one who had arrived earlier did not want to share and eat together with the other man.

He said, "Uyu ningala nayo yayi ine ndi Muzereza" meaning "I can't share food with this one because he is abnormal."

The response from the other was, "Muzereza ndiwe uku-kanirira sima yaweni" meaning "It is you who is a fool because you deny someone's food."

The row ended after giving another plate of food to the man who came second.

Rev I.M. Malongo

Rev Joseph Chimembe, author of "A Miracle", is a very gifted singer and by October 2009 had recorded two CD's of Malawian traditional worship songs.

JOYS, CHALLENGES, AND MOVING FORWARD

Kakhulajino Manse is about two and a half kilometres east of Nkhamenya trading station, near Chief Kalulama's headquarters. The old manse was built between 1963 and 1965 by Mr Chipeta under Rev Joel W Jere. Construction of the new manse was started by Mr Mithi, under Rev Glad S.M. Kumwenda, in 2005.

I came to this manse in May 2004. Since then I have been able, by the grace of God, to provide physical and spiritual comfort to the members through prayer and Bible study.

Some areas in my congregation had no drinking water, other areas had no schools. I forwarded a request to Synod office with the result that Marion Medical Mission has planted shallow wells where people now drink, and now there are schools. There are times when people around have no food; they are provided for if food is available. As in other rural areas, the manse here is known as a place where people can sell their produce; on the other hand the Christians come to present food items to the minister in the manse: the Umanyano provides maize flour every month. People always think that everything is available at the manse; this thought has endangered life in the manse in that robbers have taken advantage of this: they come pretending that they are in great need, but are just lying. If you sympathise with them you may find later that money has gone. There are times when a genuine needy person comes with hope that he will be assisted but unfortunately the request is not available.

If I say "Sorry, I do not have, therefore I cannot provide," to his understanding it is a lie.

God provides and guides; in every situation God's hand is upon us if we trust and obey Him. In interacting with the people, I am not isolated from them.

The old manse has been renovated throughout the years but still has dangerous cracks on the walls, leaking heavily when the rain comes: when it rains you become busy shifting things from one place to another to avoid the leaks; in the process some articles are damaged by the moving or destroyed directly by raindrops. Because of the large cracks, the house is in great danger of falling down. It is a very worrisome situation with the life of children and elderly people at stake. In the heavy rains the house becomes surrounded by water that reaches fifty centimetres above the ground; when going outside to the kitchen and other places you have to put off your shoes and raise your trousers. The minister's work is badly affected.

The roof is in great danger of being blown off by the wind; in the dry season a lot of dust comes through the roof to the extent that there is no difference between old and new things in the house – all are covered in dust.

Other things besides rain and dust come through the cracks. Many nyere come through the cracks in the roof and the floor. One night when we were sleeping at midnight, our first born knocked on our bedroom door: He was crying. When we let him in he said that the ants entered one of his ears and his eardrum was at risk of being destroyed. We thank God that the ants were removed from the ear without causing any damage! We rejoice in God in all things at all times! (Ephesians 5v20)

It is generally believed that the calling is for the minister and not the wife and children but in conditions such as these it becomes difficult for all members of the family. For me, in all circumstances that we have come through, my wife, Thocco Nkhula, has been a source of comfort and encouragement. The fruit of her direction and encouragement is that a new manse is under construction. The idea was discussed at session and passed.

Before the building project started, a building committee was formed to plan the project. Chairman Mr Robson Manda; Secretary Mr Aubern Mtonga; Vice-Secretary Jane Kulumbi (Mrs. Kayira); Treasurer, Mr Bester Mwale.

The Christians made 140,000 mud bricks, carried them to the site and contributed MK 100 each per year. The project started on 5th August 2005. When we were starting, we could not dream that we would reach where we are today. We have done well: erecting, roofing, plastering: all great and commendable work. I would not be fair to fail in acknowledging people for their financial, material support and encouragement: Rev L.N. Nyondo (Synod Moderator), Presbyterian Church in Ireland through Rev N.M. Nkhoma (General Secretary), my wife Thocco Nkhula, Mr R.J. Banda (session clerk), Mr Robson Banda (carpenter and building committee chairman), Mr Mithi (builder), Mr Levi Jere, Mr Winston Mwawaungulu, Mr and Mrs. P.B. Mwale, Senior Chief Kaluluma, Hon. M.M. Mandela Shaba, all Christians in Kakhulajino congregation and all others from all over.

God is providing for the manse as He did with the Israelites. The work done is not man's own but that of God. Jeremiah was called of God and assured of His guidance and protection.

So too are we.

Rev Glad S.M.Kumwenda

THE ROBBER

In 1998 in the month of September, on a Friday, I received a visitor whom I didn't know, at Mzimba Manse. Of course a manse was meant to be a home for all visitors, known or unknown. He was a man of middle age, claiming to come from my husband's home village, Chirambo. He even mentioned my husband's grandmother, whom I knew personally. He told me that his father had sent him ahead to Mzimba so that they could meet up there the following day. I was alone in the manse with children only. My husband had gone to his home village. Later on that day the man went for a walk to the market at the trading centre. While he was there I received a phone call. The voice was of a man: "Mama Mliska, may my son please stay with you? I will not be able to come tomorrow but instead I will come on Monday."

I accepted the request. When the stranger came back I told him that his father had called and I explained about the expected journey on Monday.

He looked to be a very nice man, full of responsibility. On Saturday, he went to buy drugs for my chickens because they were infected. He treated my chickens very well. He asked for a Bible and Hymn Book, which I gave him. On Sunday he attended the English Church service; we were together the rest of the day. He was a good companion to my children.

The manse at Mzimba had three bedrooms. One, where my guest was accommodated, was just opposite the sitting room. To the other bedrooms there was a corridor where there was also a bathroom and toilet.

On Monday morning, as a teacher, I went to school. At that time I was pregnant almost seven months. I locked my bedroom and put the key at a safe place in the bathroom. The visitor was at home alone; my fifth born son, Kachepa, was at nursery school. Around eleven a.m. the man went to the nursery to collect Kachepa and took him to the woman who was the manse helper. When I came back from school I was tired and decided to rest a while before starting to cook. I decided to sit outside the house and after resting there for some time I realised that I had not seen my visitor; I looked outside and inside the house. He was not there but my bedroom, which had been locked, was now wide open. My heart sank as I rushed into the bedroom, to discover that everything was in disorder and many things had been stolen: a briefcase belonging to my husband which contained his degree certificate and other valuable items, bed sheets, food items, a bag with money. That money came from friends who had been consoling us upon the death of my older brother. According to our culture this money is held for a month after the burial of the deceased.

The most terrible thing, which really frightened me, was the equipment he had taken, which I knew he would use if I found him stealing in our house: the panga knives which I kept under the bed were gone. These panga knives we used when cutting dry maize in order to put it in a heap. He had placed a bottle of cooking oil on my bed as well as the bed he had been sleeping on: I believe his plan would have been to spray oil on my eyes to prevent me seeing him. I did not know if his man would have killed or wounded me. After taking whatever he wanted he also took the keys of the front outside door. When I had discovered all this I decided to go down to the nursery to check if my son was well. The teachers told me that my visitor had collected Kachepa: my heart was broken thinking that the man might harm him. It was such a relief to find my son safe at the home of the manse caretaker.

After all of this I tried to make a follow-up call to the man's relatives.

They said, "We're sorry: that man started stealing when he was very young."

The robber was very provocative; after two days he called the manse number, asking if the stolen things were found. At first I did not recognise his voice so I answered him.

He simply said, "Keep on investigating."

I realised then that he was the one calling so I stopped answering him. This call gave me the thought that perhaps he himself was the one who had called on the Saturday, pretending to be the father. I then remembered he had asked me for the manse mobile number.

All this happened while Kachepa, my husband, was at his home village. From that time Kachepa's parents advised me not to give refuge to strangers who had no proof of identity. The congregation agreed that any stranger who would come to the manse needing help should be booked at the nearest guesthouse with the congregation responsible for paying the bills.

Mama Mliska Mughogho

Shore of Lake Malawi

WEDDING CELEBRATIONS

The year 1998 was a very interesting time for the manse at Mzimba, where I served for 5 years, from 1995 to 2000.

An orphan youth was engaged to a young girl. The youth was expected to meet all the necessary steps to wed. First he would have to pay the lobola (bride price), in full, to the family of the girl: three cattle or the equivalent in cash. The youth was handicapped since he was an orphan. He could not pay. The minister and the elders intervened by taking the role of go-between with the two families; they negotiated with the parents of the girl until the parents agreed to receive the price of one cow, which the church helped to pay.

The first challenge was through but now there was the need of the wedding ceremony costs: hire of wedding dress, a wedding hall, D.J. for entertainment and a restaurant; wedding cloth must be bought for the wedding group; cards to be printed. All this would be too expensive for the boy or even the church. The minister, the session officers and the manse committee sat down to discuss the wedding ceremony. It was agreed by all parties that the wedding celebrations would be held at the manse. The church agreed that the Christians would contribute food stuff and cooks as well as plates. The youth of the church would make a temporary shelter for the bride and groom. Church members offered all attire for the wedding group, but the wedding rings were bought by the young groom himself.

On the wedding day, representatives of both the bride and the groom came in large numbers. I married the young couple and all the wedding party came to the manse as the reception hotel. The manse was the reception hall, venue for the celebrations, home for the bride and bridegroom with the minister as the spiritual parent for both.

That wedding was a blessing to our family in the manse; we felt that we contributed to the well being, care and support of the Kingdom of God. The Christians were brought closer to the life of the manse and felt part and parcel of the ministry of Jesus Christ together with their minister. For non-Christians, they saw the care and support of the Church of Jesus Christ and the unity of God's people. The wedding couple felt humbled and blessed by the awesome support shown by the Christian community and indeed by the manse.

This story is told, then and always, by the couple, the members of the church and me, who witnessed the function. I am still in touch with the couple and there is a warm bond between us.

Rev K.T.R. Mughogho

GLOSSARY

CONGA: A dance in which people line up one behind the other, holding on to each other's shoulders or waists.

DERRY: Short for LONDONDERRY.

DURAN DURAN: Duran Duran is an English pop band that formed in Birmingham in 1978. They were part of the New Romantic Youth Fashion Movement that peaked in the United Kingdom during the early 1980s. The band members moved away from New Romanticism, working with fashion designers to establish a distinctive, elegant look.

FLAX: Flax is a pretty true-blue flowering plant, which is harvested in August, 100 days after sowing. Its fibres are separated and spun into thread which is used to weave linen cloth. Linen making was a very important Irish industry; by the end of the 18th century, linen made up half of the total exported goods from Ireland. Irish linen was exported to all over the world. Traditionally, the whole family got involved in the process. Men were usually responsible for seeding while women took charge of weeding as the flax plants grew. Reducing the weeds encouraged vigorous growth of the flax, and meant the stem was more likely to grow upright. When it was about one metre high, the plant was ready for harvest, an operation that usually involved all adults and older children.

JIGGERS: The female sand flea (Tunga Penetrans) is also known as a jigger. Jiggers embed themselves in the skin where they feed on the flesh and blood of their host. Jiggers thrive where there are few made roads, dirt floors and animals mixing freely with people.

KAROO: A semi-desert region of South Africa. The great English poet Thomas Hardy wrote in his poem *The Dead Drummer*:
Young Hodge the Drummer never knew -
Fresh from his Wessex home -
The meaning of the broad Karoo,
The Bush, the dusty loam,
And why uprose to nightly view
Strange stars amid the gloam.

KHONDI: A veranda at the front of the house.

MALAWI: (formerly known as Nyasaland) Malawi is a small African country located between Zambia, Tanzania and Mozambique. The country is about 900 km long and 150 km wide at its widest part. Malawi has no ocean coastline, but the third largest lake in Africa covers almost one fifth of Malawi. It is Lake Malawi: Lake Malawi has more species of fish than any other inland body of water in the world, with a total of over 500.

MAMA MLISKA: The term used in Malawi for the wife of a Presbyterian Minister.

MANSE: The word "manse" is defined in the English dictionary as "(in some denominations) the house provided for a minister" derived from two Latin words: mansus – dwelling; manere – to stay.

NGONI: The Ngoni people are an ethnic group living in Malawi, Mozambique, Tanzania and Zambia in east-central Africa. The Ngoni trace their origins to the Zulu people in South Africa. On the high plateau in the small country of Malawi, the Ngoni settled and made their home in the mid nineteenth century. This central African country became the new home for the Ngoni people after their forty-year journey from Natal to Tanganyika.

PRESBYTERIANS: Presbyterian theology typically emphasizes the sovereignty of God, the authority of the Scriptures, and the necessity of grace through faith in Christ. The roots of Presbyterianism lie in the European Reformation of the 16th century, the leadership of John Calvin being particularly influential. Local congregations are governed by elders (in Greek, *presbuteroi*) who take part in local pastoral care and decision-making at all levels.

ROBERT BURNS: Robert Burns (25 January 1759 – 21 July 1796) was a Scottish poet. He is widely regarded as the national poet of Scotland, and is acclaimed worldwide. He is the best known of the poets who have written in the Scots language, although he also wrote much in English and a Scots dialect. Two of Burns' most famous and best loved poems are: "Auld Lang Syne" and "To a Mouse"

RONDAVEL: A traditional African-style house. The rondavel is usually round or oval in shape and is traditionally made with materials that can be locally found in raw form.

SHIRE: The Shire is a river in Malawi and Mozambique. The river has been known as the Shiré or Chire River. It is the outlet of Lake Malawi and flows into the Zambezi. The upper Shire River connects Lake Malawi with Lake Malombe. The river's valley is part of the Great Rift Valley system.

TSUNAMI: A tsunami or tidal wave is a series of water waves. Because of the immense volumes of water and energy involved, tsunamis can devastate coastal regions. Casualties can be high because the waves move faster than humans can run.

UMANYANO: An organisation for women within the Presbyterian Church in Malawi. The women wear a black and white uniform and meet regularly for prayer and Bible Study as well as visiting and giving help to sick and needy people in their area.